PRAISE FOR STEVE MILLER AND *UNCOPYABLE*

"Miller is a marketing guru who teaches practical, common-sense lessons to help you stand out, give you a competitive advantage, and help make you…Uncopyable!"

—**Shep Hyken**, CSP, CPAE;
best-selling author, *The Amazement Revolution*

"I love books that disturb conventional thinking. Steve Miller nails the pivotal, counterintuitive point about achieving sustainable success—don't compete, be Uncopyable. *Uncopyable* is a must-read for any small-business owner who wants to avoid the typical pitfalls and emerge as a game-changer business to be reckoned with."

—**Art Turock**, elite performance game changer;
author, *Competent Is Not an Option*

"Real innovation is hard. I've spent four decades fighting to move business owners past the 'marketing incest' that occurs when they are competition-centric in their thinking. And it is about thinking before it can be about anything else—including growth, sustainability, and profit. In *Uncopyable*, Steve provides a clear challenge to the way a person presently thinks about his business. Now that copycatting occurs at the speed of light and classic price-and-profit protections are disintegrating, what Steve describes as the Uncopyable Mind-Set is more vital than ever."

—**Dan S. Kennedy**, direct marketing strategist/copywriter;
author of the *No B.S.* series, including *No B.S. Price Strategy*
(www.NoBSBooks.com)

"Everyone wants a competitive advantage, but not everyone knows how to do it. *Uncopyable* changes that by providing practical strategies and tools explained using contemporary examples and intriguing stories. Read it to get an edge over the competition."

—**Mark Sanborn**, best-selling author, *The Fred Factor*

"Steve Miller is the master of marketing and a legend in the consulting world. In *Uncopyable* he argues successfully what it takes to be extraordinary in the ever-changing, highly competitive global sphere."

—**Nido R. Qubein**, president, High Point University

"I don't make recommendations or endorsements lightly. But, as I've told readers of my newsletter, if you have any responsibility for sales and marketing in your organization, you owe it to yourself to seek Steve out. He's provided us with clear, actionable marketing steps and ideas resulting in a 56 percent year-to-date increase in subscription revenue. I can't wait to see the completed version of his new book, *Uncopyable*. It's a whole new way of thinking about marketing in a competitive world that puts the reader on the road to dominance."

—**Pete Harris**, co-owner, Incisive Computing Solutions, LLC

"Not so long ago, if you had great marketing or spectacular customer service or cheap web traffic or some other slight edge, you were reasonably secure against competition. Today, however, they're drilling subterranean tunnels and infiltrating your basement even as we speak. You need a substantial edge. Steve Miller has applied his mind to the question of how you can become Uncopyable."

—**Perry Marshall**, author, *80/20 Sales & Marketing;*
Ultimate Guide to Google AdWords; and *Evolution 2.0*

"If anyone has the right to teach us how to be Uncopyable, it is Steve Miller. He has modeled the strategies in his breakthrough book for more than twenty-five years. He goes beyond branding and innovation, which, though valuable, always leave us competing. World class is good, but world class and Uncopyable is better! This book gives you both 'whats' and 'how-tos.'"

—**Bob Pike**, CPLP Fellow, CSP, CPAE, founder/chairman, P3 Associates, LLC; founder/editor, Training and Performance Forum

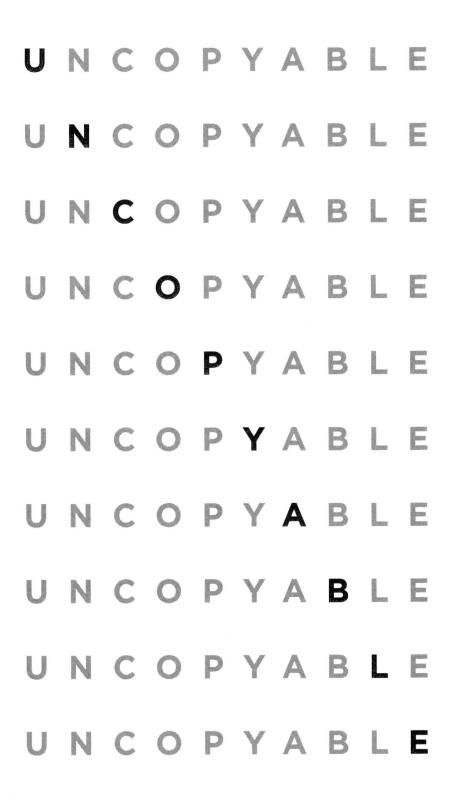

_ER

UNCOPYABLE

HOW TO CREATE AN

UNFAIR ADVANTAGE OVER YOUR

COMPETITION

Advantage®

Published by Advantage, Charleston, South Carolina.
Member of Advantage Media Group.

ADVANTAGE is a registered trademark, and the Advantage colophon is a trademark of Advantage Media Group, Inc.

Printed in the United States of America.

ISBN: 978-1-59932-787-7
LCCN: 2016963093

Cover design by Katie Biondo.

This publication is designed to provide accurate and authoritative information in regard to the subject matter covered. It is sold with the understanding that the publisher is not engaged in rendering legal, accounting, or other professional services. If legal advice or other expert assistance is required, the services of a competent professional person should be sought.

Advantage Media Group is proud to be a part of the Tree Neutral® program. Tree Neutral offsets the number of trees consumed in the production and printing of this book by taking proactive steps such as planting trees in direct proportion to the number of trees used to print books. To learn more about Tree Neutral, please visit **www.treeneutral.com.**

Advantage Media Group is a publisher of business, self-improvement, and professional development books. We help entrepreneurs, business leaders, and professionals share their Stories, Passion, and Knowledge to help others Learn & Grow. Do you have a manuscript or book idea that you would like us to consider for publishing? Please visit **advantagefamily.com** or call **1.866.775.1696.**

To my girls.
Still keeping my promise!

TABLE OF CONTENTS

Let me tell you something you already know.

Competition is fierce.

What keeps you up at night? If your one-word answer is "competition," you're right to be worried. Competition is a huge challenge to every industry around the world, and it gets more cutthroat every year as more businesses battle for a slice of the pie.

There is a remedy for your sleeplessness, though—not just a new way to outpace your competition but a way in which to render the whole notion of competition toothless and irrelevant. It's a fix that's simultaneously blindingly simple and brain-meltingly complex.

Ready?

You need to be Uncopyable.

You're stuck in the crazy hamster wheel of positioning your company against your competition. You come up with a product improvement that's clearly better than theirs. Victory! But the next day or the day after that, they come back with an improvement on your improvement. So you put your nose to the grindstone to come up with a new and improved improvement. And they follow up with something just slightly better than yours. Hear that clattering sound? They're on the same kind of hamster wheel you are, and it's a race nobody wins.

The problem with the hamster-wheel approach is it's based on becoming *better* than the competition. But you don't want to be better, because better can always be bettered, ad infinitum. The only way to climb off of the wheel is by becoming Uncopyable—demonstrably, clearly, undoubtedly, measurably, meaningfully Uncopyable. You just haven't figured out how that works yet.

But many companies *have* figured it out. Interestingly, none of them achieved their dominant positions in highly competitive marketplaces through unique, demonstrably superior products, but I'm betting you've heard of them.

Disneyland and Disney World are Uncopyable. Disney's theme parks are extremely well-designed amusement parks. There are plenty of other well-designed amusement parks around the world, but Disney doesn't really sell amusement parks. It sells theme parks wrapped in amazing, once-in-a-lifetime experiences.

Harley-Davidson is Uncopyable. Harley-Davidson sells motorcycles. Its bikes aren't necessarily unique or superior to those of its competitors. But, of course, Harley-Davidson doesn't actually sell motorcycles. It sells membership to an exclusive, tightly knit community—almost a tribal experience.

The American Girl store is Uncopyable. And the American Girl store sells dolls. I'm pretty sure you can find other dolls (hello, Barbie), but the American Girl store doesn't truly sell dolls. It sells girl power: increased self-esteem, confidence, and sometimes, historically based educational experiences girls want to share with their friends.

Have these giants achieved their positions with lower prices? That would be a big "Duh, no." A day pass for Disney World is over $100. An American Girl doll starts at around $150 (hey, it comes with a paperback!) and the entry-level Harley will set you back about $7k, twice if you want a real "hog." So why do people line up, waving fistfuls of money every time a new ride or model or character doll is introduced?

Each of these companies occupies a unique position in its marketplace, one for which their competitors would gladly sell their firstborn male sons. And each has carefully managed to develop an almost unbreakable relationship with their most highly qualified targets.

And they've done all this in highly competitive markets.

But these are huge, well-known brands, you might be thinking. *I don't have the deep pockets and resources they have to separate our company from the competition!*

Well, have you heard of these companies?

- Stor-Loc

- Incisive Computing

- Sunriver Brewing Company

- Strictly Bicycles

- Cafe Sintra

No? These are all small businesses, maybe smaller than yours, which have all achieved a highly unique and desirable competitive position in their respective industries. In one manner or other, they're all Uncopyable.

Take Fabletics: cofounded by actress Kate Hudson, Fabletics has exploded on the $44-billion, active-wear scene, reaching $200 million in just two and a half years.[1] How? Having star credibility is all well and good, but it's the business model Fabletics has built that really makes the difference. By constantly updating its colors, textures, and prints, Fabletics creates whole, themed, fitness wardrobes. It's fast fashion from design to delivery in eight weeks.

But where the company really breaks the mold is in *how* it sells. Instead of the typical online retail store that simply offers a line of merchandise, Fabletics sells a monthly subscription. Paying subscribers get discounts. New collections are released the first of every month, but with plenty of incentives offered between cycles to lure shoppers. But if you stop your subscription, you won't be the first to see the latest fashions. You're out of the loop. Fabletics doesn't just sell clothing. It sells membership to the young, fit-fashion lifestyle— the opportunity to have a new, up-to-the-minute look, style, and positive self-expression experience every month.

---

1   "Dressing down: The rise of Athleisure," CBS News, May 22, 2016, http://www.cbsnews.com/news/dressing-down-the-rise-of-athleisure/.

THE THREE TRADITIONAL
COMPONENTS OF COMPETITION

For years, business advisors, college professors, and authors have taught us there are three basic components of competitive difference:

1.   You could have a better *product.*

2.   You could have a better *price.*

3.   You could have better *service.*

We could create a competitive strategy based on only two of those components, we were told, but it wasn't possible to have all three. Great product plus low price? Super, but you couldn't afford to deliver awesome service too. Great product plus awesome service? Fantastic, but you needed to charge a high price to achieve those. What about low price and awesome service? It was rare but possible. Unfortunately, you'd have to sacrifice great product, maybe via lower-quality manufacturing or by using poorer-quality materials, in order to maintain awesome service. But no matter how you sliced it, two out of three was the best you could hope for.

Do you believe that formula still holds true?

Of course you don't! Technology's advances and, in particular, the Internet and computing power, have effectively erased any chance of creating and producing a unique product. Your products or services are very similar to what your competitors offer, and it's getting harder and harder to differentiate.

A 2014 study, "Escaping the Commodity Trap," by Roland Berger and the International Controller Association (ICV) shows standardized products are impacting prices and margins, thus threatening companies in all industries.

The study states:

Almost all industries today are struggling with the increasing commoditization of their products and services. This is putting considerable pressure on prices and margins and leads to fiercer competition. And not only the mass market is being affected: even more complex and innovative products are subject to increasingly technical and qualitative standardization. The upshot is that new market players are getting more and more competitive while established providers are successively becoming interchangeable. The study shows 63% of the companies surveyed are already facing the commoditization of their products and services, yet 54% have yet to take sufficient action to escape. At many companies, there is a significant gap between recognizing the commodity trap and reacting accordingly.[2]

Maybe you think you *are* different from your competition. You just can't understand why your customers and prospects don't see it as clearly as you do, because it seems you're always forced to compete on price, which really hurts your profits because you can't get the margins you'd like to have.

Okay, I'll play. Answer this question for me: Why do your customers do business with you? You know what? I already know your answer. Your customers do business with you because you have the *best* people who deliver the *best* customer service in your marketplace! I know that's what you're thinking because that's what you're saying on your websites, in your brochures, and in your videos. And that's not good enough, because your competition is saying the exact same thing.

---

2   Roland Berger Strategy Consultants, "The Commodity Trap," April 2014, https://www.rolandberger.com/en/press/Press-Release-Details_5589.html.

The problem with the phrase "customer service" is it's just a buzzy catchphrase that sounds very professional yet it has no definitive meaning. It's a vague generality. Your definition of customer service might be (and probably is) completely different from what your customers think it is.

Yet, you say you deliver great customer service. Every single one of your competitors also claims to deliver great customer service. The guy mowing your yard says he delivers great customer service. Even United Airlines and Comcast say they deliver great customer service!

Think about it. What *exactly* do you mean when you say you deliver great customer service? Do you mean you deliver your products on time? Fantastic, but isn't that what you're supposed to do? If you promise to deliver on a certain date and you do it, what makes it so great?

Do you make ordering your product easy? Do you answer the phone quickly? Do you promptly resolve a problem or issue when one comes up? Aren't we supposed to do all that? Shouldn't these things be the expected level of service? When and how did they become competitive advantages?

I was recently preparing for a keynote speech at a large automotive aftermarket distributor meeting in Dallas. I took the opportunity to visit with a couple of distributors near me in Seattle. In one conversation, the owner was talking about how he wanted his distributorship to be known for its world-class customer service. He cited an example of his wife calling their bank with a question: "A human being answered the phone! My wife was amazed. *That's* what we're going to do! We're going to answer the phone!"

While I understood his enthusiasm for this groundbreaking idea, I couldn't help but think back to when *everybody* answered the phone. We had to! There was no other option. Now, as technology develops new and "better" ways for us to communicate (or to not communicate), this method of communicating with customers has magically gone from yesterday's technology to the new competitive advantage. Amazing.

Of course, it's just a matter of time before his competitors copy that too. He and they are trapped on the hamster wheel. How did he get stuck there, and how can he (and you) get off it?

THE THREE TRAPS

Trap #1: Commoditization

When we talk about commoditization, we're usually talking about the deliverable: the product or service we provide. Most of us stubbornly believe that, somehow, the product we bring to the table is unique but, of course, that's almost never true. All moms and dads think their children are special. Too many fathers even see their sons or daughters as the next Tiger Woods, Serena Williams, or LeBron James. No, they aren't. As a businessperson, your deliverable is *your* kid, and chances are, your view of your product's uniqueness is as skewed as Dad's. This view—that your deliverable is more unique than it is, or it will stay that way—is one of the three elements that can push you into what I call the commodity trap. For this fact, blame technology.

I've read we've seen more advancement in our knowledge and technology in the last twenty years than in all mankind's history to date. My incredibly beautiful/smart/witty twenty-four-year-old daughter, Kelly, never experienced:

- black Ma Bell hard-wired telephones attached to the wall

- cars without seat belts or air conditioners

- three-on-the-tree

- handwritten letters as the norm, not the exception

- nightly news from Walter Cronkite or Huntley and Brinkley

- no remote (Although my dad always said he had a remote: "Steve, get your butt off the couch and change that channel. It's time for *Candid Camera*!")

Technology's relentless forward march has come with a cost, especially for you, the small businessperson. It used to be a business could develop a new or a vastly improved product and enjoy a competitive advantage for many months, sometimes even years. It wasn't just that patents protected new products. It was because it was just so darn hard to copy them! Today, it's so easy to copy a new and/or improved product that it's difficult, if not impossible, to create and maintain Uncopyable products.

I played a peripheral role in the launch of the Swiffer WetJet mop back in 2001. It was supposed to be a game changer in the household-cleaning category. And it was—for a few weeks. Competitors quickly came out with their own versions of the Swiffer WetJet and, in short order, it was no longer unique. If it hadn't been for the marketing intelligence and muscle Proctor & Gamble had, who knows whether it would still be around. How many other new and briefly unique products have been introduced since then, only to be quickly copied? I frequently hear an audience member or consulting client lament, "We created this really great new product, and the damn competition stole it!" But they're missing the bigger point: the very idea of developing a new and unique product today, producing it, and having a long-term advantage is laughable.

That's the new reality, gang. In today's world, if something *can* be copied, it *will* be copied.

You don't want that. You don't want to be copyable. You want to escape the bonds of commoditi-

IF SOMETHING *CAN* BE COPIED, IT *WILL* BE COPIED.

zation. And that requires a new approach, a new way of thinking about competition and your relationship with your customers.

Trap #2: Competitive Strategy

Take a look at industries such as hotels, automobiles, airlines, and even fast-food restaurants. Narrow your focus down to the top players in each of those industries. Usually, there are around six.

Now, study their strategies. What do you see? Odds are you see a common strategy, a strategic orthodoxy, if you will. The leaders tend to look alike and act alike. Which hotel chain first offered coffee makers in its rooms? Odds are you don't know (I think it was Holiday Inn, but I can't prove it).

And how many hotel rooms have coffee makers today? All of them!

What about the more recent "benefit" of curved shower rods in the bathrooms? Who started that? In fact, it was the Westin Hotel chain, thanks to the then Westin SVP Sue Brush, who was sent a catalogue photo of the rod by an employee, which she sent on to Westin's CEO Barry Sternlicht.[3] Today, most hotels rooms offer curved shower rods.

Why does this happen? It's because all the hotels chains watch each other closely. In fact, I would venture to say all the hotel chains spend most of their marketing and brainstorming time studying the competition. "Hey, Westin just introduced a thing called the

---

3   Marketing Immortals, "Sue Brush," http://marketingimmortals.com/categories/corporate-client/sue-brush/.

heavenly bed. *We* can do that—and even better than them! We'll offer a Sleep Number bed!"

Admit it or not, your industry, whether it's B2B (business to business) or B2C (business to consumer), is like that, too.

Over the last thirty years, I've spoken at, and consulted for, organizations in 126 different industries. The variety amazes me—manufacturing, construction, food, portable storage, website design, oil and gas, candy, health care, soft drink, coffee, fitness, toys, automotive aftermarket—the list is long. While most of my work is in the B2B world, I've noticed there are some common practices among all industries, regardless of whether they're B2B or B2C.

As I already pointed out, every industry practices a common strategic orthodoxy. It doesn't come by accident. It comes by heuristics. If you work in the manufacturing industry, for example, you live in a manufacturing-centric community. Many, if not most, of your friends are also in manufacturing. You spend most of your time thinking about manufacturing. You probably attend manufacturing trade shows such as the International Manufacturing Technology Show, East-Tec, and maybe Hannover Messe. You read manufacturing trade magazines such as *Machine Shop*. Mostly, you spend your workdays surrounded by coworkers who think, eat, drink, and sleep manufacturing. You all talk about the product or service you provide the industry. You talk about suppliers, customers, and competition.

It's your world.

In the same way you're focused on manufacturing, others live in the candy world. They have friends and acquaintances in the candy industry. They attend the Sweets & Snacks Expo and read *Candy Industry* magazine. They talk about suppliers, customers, and competitors, all with similar behavior. But your worlds don't cross over much, if at all. You don't attend the Sweets & Snacks Expo, and they don't attend the International Manufacturing Technology Show. This is also true for the countless other "worlds" in which people live and work. So when you or your company wants to innovate, where do you get new ideas? Not from the candy industry, that's for sure. You look within your world. It's only natural because that's the heuristic we've developed.

And that's a mistake.

To be sure, you need to keep an eye on the competition. If someone else does add an improvement such as a curved shower rod, you need to bring your game up a notch too, even if it just means copying. After all, your target market will always base its minimum level of expectation on the best thing being offered in your industry. You might even be able to improve on that new feature your competition introduced—"More of the same but better," as my friend Art Turock says.

However, "better" is temporary. Within a given industry, competitors are like a circular parade of processionary caterpillars, with the head of one caterpillar following the butt of the caterpillar directly in front. They're all following the caterpillar ahead of them for new ideas. As I said, if it can be copied, everybody will copy it. As a result, competition doesn't breed innovation. *Competition breeds conformity.*

COMPETITION DOESN'T BREED INNOVATION. *COMPETITION BREEDS CONFORMITY.*

The bad news is this behavior is common practice. The good news is it's actually pretty easy to step out of the parade.

Competitive strategy can be used to create meaningful difference between you and your competition, but not if you just watch them for "new" ideas. Developing an Uncopyable advantage requires creating a strategy with new, contrarian eyes—looking at your industry, your competitors, and especially your customers, through a different filter.

Trap #3: Price Pressure

When people consider a purchase, whether of a product or a service, they weigh their perception of the different values offered to them by potential suppliers. We all instinctively know value is something more than price, but often, as suppliers, we have difficulty explaining why *our* value is better than *their* price.

And that's a bad thing.

When prospective customers cannot differentiate between two products on the basis of performance and quality, they look at the producing companies' quality of service. If they can't tell the difference between the companies' levels of service, they have only one point of differentiation left: price. We don't want that to happen. We don't want to compete on price, because that's a losing battle.

So how do you achieve Uncopyable Superiority? What's the secret code so many companies struggle to break?

In a word—*attachment*: your customer's attachment to you.

For many years, business experts, authors, and speakers have sold us on the importance of creating passionately loyal customers. We're told we've got to inspire evangelists and promoters who will proudly carry our Kool-Aid out into the world.

But there's something fundamentally wrong with that perspective: it's *our* perspective. We, the supplier, look at this situation through *our* eyes. We want *loyalty*. We want *evangelists*. We want *promoters*. It's all well and good for us to want these things, but to make them our goal is putting the cart before the horse. Loyalty doesn't spring out of nowhere. Something important has to happen before it's inspired.

People don't initially buy products or services with the intention of developing a relationship with the producer—and certainly not with the idea of becoming evangelists for the producer!

Our customers must first become *attached* to us, professionally and personally attached. That's a tall order, but attachment is the key to everything that follows: the loyalty, the evangelism, and the promotion of what you sell by those to whom you sell it. When you create attachment, you not only best your competition but also leave them scratching their heads and eating your dust.

This book will teach you how to grab and hold the unfair advantage—how to become Uncopyable.

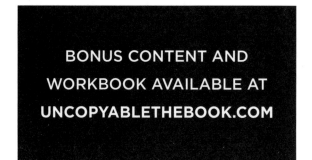

BONUS CONTENT AND
WORKBOOK AVAILABLE AT
UNCOPYABLETHEBOOK.COM

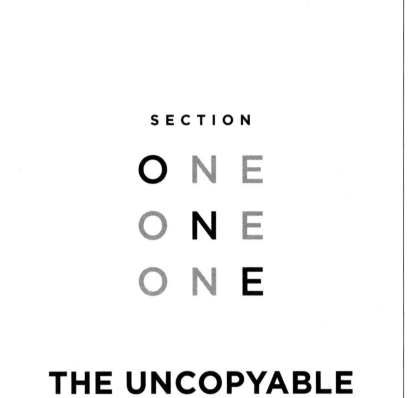

SECTION

ONE
ONE
ONE

THE UNCOPYABLE FOUNDATION

CHAPTER ONE

The Uncopyable System

(What You Will Learn in This Book)

The Pulitzer-Prize winning musical *Hamilton* is a Broadway phenom-
enon, a true force of nature achieving an Uncopyable Attachment
with its fans. Nominated for a record-setting sixteen Tony Awards, it
won eleven, along with the 2016 Grammy for Best Musical Theater
Album. As of this writing, the Broadway show is sold out for the
next twenty-three months, but for only twenty-three months because
tickets for performances beyond that date haven't been released yet!
Its life in New York City and around the world is virtually guaranteed
for years to come.

It's true many other plays and musicals have developed raving
fans. *The Phantom of the Opera*, *Chicago*, and *The Lion King* are the
three longest-running Broadway shows of all time. I was a huge fan of
the fourth longest-running show, *Cats*, seeing it the first time shortly
after it opened in New York City, and three more times including
the London production with my smoking-hot wife, Kay. I loved that
show! It sold out performances for a long time.

There have been other shows achieving that status of hottest
ticket in town, but not a lot. *The Book of Mormon* became an impossible ticket to get for quite a while after its 2011 debut. Since the

1918 comedy *Lightnin'* first broke the barrier of one thousand performances, only 114 shows have achieved that number.[4] *Hamilton* is
today's hot ticket. But it's also much more.

In the June 2016 edition of *Fast Company* magazine, Rachel
Syme put it best when she wrote:

> *Hamilton, which opened in the Richard Rogers Theatre
> in August 2015, after an off-Broadway run, isn't just a
> hit musical. It's one of those rare cultural phenomena that
> reaches beyond its genre and infiltrates the broader conversa-
> tion. Fourth graders love the show as much as 80-year-olds.
> Hip-hop fans and history buffs alike are giddy over its inspi-
> rational, intricately rhymed retelling of the founding fathers'
> complicated relationships with Aaron Burr, George Washing-
> ton, Thomas Jefferson, and more.*[5]

Lin-Manuel Miranda, creator, composer, lyricist, and original
star of *Hamilton* has developed a fan base and relationship with those
hundreds of thousands of fans who haven't seen and may never see
the show. Beyond the obvious cast album and obligatory social media
participation, Miranda has engaged fans through other nontraditional means. From the beginning, in previews, Miranda established
a daily lottery of two dozen, $10, front-row seats, which continues
today. Fans line up early every day in hopes of grabbing one of the
hallowed golden tickets. It has become known as Ham4Ham. As
Hamilton grew in prominence, crowds became huge. Knowing most
of those fans wouldn't get a ticket, Miranda and other cast members

---

4   "List of the longest-running Broadway shows," Wikipedia, accessed November 2,
2016, https://en.wikipedia.org/wiki/List_of_the_longest-running_Broadway_shows.

5   Rachel Syme, "How 'Hamilton' Creator Lin-Manuel Miranda Is Building A Brand
For The Ages," *Fast Company*, May 16, 2016, https://www.fastcompany.com/3058967/
most-creative-people/how-hamilton-creator-lin-manuel-miranda-is-building-a-
brand-for-the-age.

launched a series of impromptu short performances and videos as a thank-you and to keep the crowds calm on sweltering days. These performances took on a life of their own. They are broadcast on YouTube and include guest performers from other Broadway shows.

In 2015, Miranda was approached by the Gilder Lehrman Institute for American History about creating a new curriculum initiative. Backed by a $1.46 million grant from the Rockefeller Foundation, twenty thousand eleventh-grade students in New York City Title I schools will each pay just a "Hamilton" ($10) to see the performance and then integrate Alexander Hamilton into classroom studies.

Dissecting a *tour de force* such as *Hamilton* helps us understand how it achieved current Uncopyable status.

THE UNCOPYABLE MIND-SET

Shortly before the sports pop-culture site Grantland shut down, Rempert Browne interviewed Miranda about his past and how he developed *Hamilton*. At one point Browne asks, "When it comes down to it, if you had to pinpoint one thing, is it making musicals? Is it telling stories? Is it filling in the gaps of American and New York history?"

Miranda replies, "It's interesting, I think of it as, what's the thing that's not in the world that should be in the world?"[6]

That's an Uncopyable Mind-Set: looking at something everybody else sees but seeing something different.

---

6   Rembert Browne, "Genius: A Conversation With 'Hamilton' Maestro Lin-Manuel Miranda," Grantland, September 29, 2015, http://grantland.com/hollywood-prospectus/genius-a-conversation-with-hamilton-maestro-lin-manuel-miranda/.

Oftentimes, in my own interviews, I'll be asked to synopsize all this into a sound bite. My reply is, "Look at what everybody else is doing and don't do it."

Simple advice—but not easy to do. We all have our heuristics, outside influences, perceptions, and opinions about things. They're drilled into us. But if we truly want to clearly separate ourselves from the crowd, this is exactly what we must do.

And being Uncopyable is a moving target. Will *Hamilton* be considered Uncopyable in ten years? Probably not, but that'll likely be a result of Miranda writing the new rules of competition for the next generation.

Tiger Woods did the same thing. When he burst onto the professional golf scene in 1996, he was expected to do very well. But nobody expected him to be, literally, unbeatable. Woods took golf to a level nobody had seen before. He was the best at almost every aspect of the game. Many golf historians feel Tiger's mental toughness was far beyond that of previous champions, but the genuinely new dynamic Woods brought to the game in which golfers had previously been seen as "not really athletes" was his physical conditioning. Outside a small handful of fitness proponents, most notably Gary Player, golfers weren't known for running ten miles and lifting weights.

Tiger's physical prowess was incredible to watch and intimidating to play against. He hit the ball farther and straighter than anybody on tour. For years when Tiger teed off in a tournament, everybody else pretty much played for second. Twenty years later, the newest generation of golfers has grown up under Tiger's new rules. They are athletes in the complete sense of the word. And nowadays, they hit it farther and straighter than Tiger ever did.

Achieving Uncopyable status requires a consciously developed practice of observation and curiosity and an almost contrarian perspective. Instead of following the leaders in your market, break away from them by creating new rules of competition they can't or won't play under—as *Hamilton* does.

And don't fall into the trap of thinking you can just ask your customers what they want that's different. I guarantee Lin-Manuel Miranda didn't do that. Your customers don't know what they want. They know they want something better—but not different.

Nobody asked for an eight-track tape player.

Nobody asked for a cell phone, let alone a smart phone.

Nobody asked for the Internet.

Nobody asked for social media.

Nobody asked for Amazon.com.

My all-time favorite quote about this came from Henry Ford: "If I'd asked people what they wanted, they would have said faster horses."

UNDERSTANDING THE TRUE MARKETING PROCESS

Do you realize you're probably approaching marketing backward? "True dat," as my friend Kelly would say.

Too many small businesses see marketing as something *else* they need to do after they've done the important stuff. And many also see marketing as a necessary evil but not really the business they're in. As a result, what often happens is they ride a revenue roller coaster. It goes something like this:

1.   When your company first started, you and your team (if you have a team) knocked on doors, made cold calls, and maybe even grabbed a directory of company names and started dialing for dollars. (On my first sales job, our sales manager threw the *Yellow Pages* at me and said, "There's your list!")

2. After a lot of these calls, you generate some sales. Everybody's happy! But then you have to fulfill the orders, so you and your team switch your efforts to production and delivery.

3. While you're focusing on fulfillment, there are no outbound sales or marketing efforts. Because there aren't, sales dry up eventually. And with no orders to fulfill, you and your team, once more, have to knock on doors, make cold calls, and maybe grab that directory again.

4. This scenario repeats itself over and over. When you're filling orders, sales are being ignored. When you have no orders to fill, you push sales. It's feast or famine. You're on the business roller coaster and you'd really like to get off, but you don't know how.

5. One day a media salesperson cold calls on you and makes a pitch: "I can expose your brand to twenty-five thousand names every week, and it'll only cost you two and a half cents each! If you make only *one* sale, it'll pay for the whole thing!" You get sucked in to the funny numbers, thinking, *Hey I can work on my business, and this will take care of the marketing for me!* Yeah, right.

6. It doesn't work. Of course, it doesn't work! So you go back onto the roller coaster, $625 poorer. Do you learn your lesson? Unfortunately, most don't. In fact, many people think, *Well, that marketing tool doesn't work!* You get back on the roller coaster, and time passes until yet another media salesperson drops in, and the scenario plays out all over again.

Why does this happen to so many small businesses? There are two simple reasons: First, *you are not in the business you think you're in.* Do you manufacture widgets? I don't care whether they're small, inexpensive widgets or big, huge, expensive widgets. You are not in the business of making widgets. You are in the business of *selling* and *marketing* widgets. The widget is incidental. It's merely the deliverable for what you're selling. Do you manufacture golf clubs? That's cool, but if you don't sell them, you're just going to end up with a big pile of steel. Do you build towering high-rise condominiums? Sweet! But if nobody occupies those skyscraper views, then you're selling to Trump—for cheap.

This is one of the most difficult lessons for small-business owners. You *love* what you do! Maybe, you grew up loving to fish. You spent years on the river or boat and are happiest when you're fishing.

One day you come up with a lure that large mouth bass just can't resist. Other fishermen notice you hit your limit every day, and they ask for the secret. You tell them about your lure, and, of course, they want you to make some for them. You start hand-making your special lures. A bunch of people buy them, and someone suggests you start a business. That's the ticket! You can make a living in the sport you love! You start a business, and next thing you know, you've got a production line, inventory, rent, and maybe even an employee or two.

Let's keep this short because we know what happens. You think you're in the business of making lures. People will naturally be attracted to them and purchase them. Easy peasy!

But that's not what happens, is it? It's not so easy peasy, is it? And the reason is you never thought you'd actually have to get out and *sell* those little buggers. Whether you like it or not, you are now in the business of *selling* and *marketing* large mouth bass lures.

The second reason for the marketing roller coaster is small-business owners think they can hire an outside resource to do the sales and marketing. Sometimes, they hire an agency. Sometimes, it's a freelancer. Sometimes, it's a sales representative. Sometimes, it's a full-time person.

It sort of makes sense to get help when you finally understand you need it. But this course actually misses a critical first step: *You (the business owner) are first and foremost the number-one salesperson for your company, and if you can't sell your product, nobody else can, either.*

History is filled with extraordinary corporate success stories, most of which are about founders and CEOs who embraced the role of being their company's top salesperson.

At the age of sixty-five and often sleeping in the back of his car, Colonel Harlan Sanders visited restaurants, offered to cook his chicken, and, if workers liked it, he'd negotiate franchise rights to his Kentucky Fried Chicken recipe then and there.

Ely Callaway Jr. bought the golf-equipment manufacturer Hickory Sticks for $400,000. In 1983, he became president and moved the company to Carlsbad, California, where he sold clubs out of his Cadillac, renaming the company, Callaway, Inc.

The first sales of Phil Knight, Nike's cofounder, were conducted out of a now-legendary, green, Plymouth Valiant automobile at track meets across the Pacific Northwest.

Major CEOs throughout history, such as Mary Kay Ash, John Patterson of NCR, Larry Ellison of Oracle, and Napolean Barragan of 1-800-Mattress, understood the importance of sales and marketing as the primary function of their businesses.[7] That's your job too.

7   "Ten Greatest Salespeople of All Time," *Inc.*, March 28, 2011, http://www.inc.com/ss/10-greatest-salespeople-of-all-time.

THE FOUNDATION BLOCKS OF UNCOPYABLE

Once business owners understand their number-one role and the true function of their company, they need to understand the correct steps for achieving the highest success, and those steps must be in the right order. The media you use—direct mail, your website, trade advertising, Val-Pak, social media, or any of the other myriad of tools available—is *not* where you start a marketing strategy.

The Marketing Diamond™

You start with your *market*. Who are the prospective customers in your target market? What can you tell me about them? There are two important parts to knowing your market: demographic and psychographic.

Demographic is usually easy for us. What industry are these customers in? Where are they located? How big is their company? How many sales? How many employees? Most of us know the answers to questions such as these, which is great because they give us the *profile* of our target, identifying our prospects.

The second part, the *message*, isn't always so easy, because we have to sort of climb inside the minds of our prospects.

What problems, challenges, obstacles, or hurdles do our target prospects face every day?

What keeps them awake at night?

What aspirations and opportunities do they have?

What have your target prospects tried to either fix pain or achieve gain that hasn't worked?

After you've painted a clear picture of your target-market prospects, what message can you craft that gets their attention? The more you can show how working with you will fix pain or achieve gain, the better chance you'll have. The best way to do this is to join the conversation already going on in the prospect's mind. A simple example is in the weight-loss industry. It's not so much that people want to lose weight but, rather, what losing that weight will achieve for them: turning heads on the beach, being the slimmest woman at the class reunion, getting a pre-pregnancy body back.

The better job you do of matching the message to your market, the more success you'll have.

The third part is the *media* you use to send your *message* to your *market*. There are, literally, hundreds, maybe thousands, of different types of media you can choose to use, but there is no one perfect medium that works for everybody. Yes, social media works for some businesses—but not all businesses. TV still works for some, no matter what you've heard. Heck, even billboards work for some businesses!

The key to finding the right media is simple: Does your target market already pay attention to it? That's it. Nothing more. I don't care if there are more people on Pinterest than live in Japan. If *my* market isn't on Pinterest, it's useless to me.

On the flip side, if I build five-axis, horizontal, milling machines and I find out my market reads *Today's Cat*, you can take it to the bank I'm advertising in *Today's Cat*.

The big question mark, of course, is *moment.* When will a lead make a decision to buy? Sometimes, we might be able to influence and speed up the decision-making process, but most of the time, we can't.

Here's the big question: When a lightning bolt comes out of the sky, striking our leads in the head and they realize they need that solution *right now*, do they think of us first? Do they think of us second? Do they think of us at all? Our goal is, in fact, to be the *only* solution they think of.

If we correctly follow the *market-message-media-moment* plan and add the Uncopyable strategies outlined in the chapters ahead, we can influence the decision when the *moment* is right.

Your Branding Strategy

Have you ever heard about the guy in Anchorage who took a set of tires to Nordstrom and asked for his money back? The salesman contacted the manager, and after some discussion, they determined this guy was a very good customer. So they refunded his money even though Nordstrom doesn't sell tires! Clearly, this is an amazing story that reinforces the Nordstrom policy of customer service and unquestioning refunds.

There's only one problem: there's no proof it's true.

It's part of the Nordstrom myth. I've heard many different versions of the story, usually from a professional speaker using it as an incredible customer-service example of just how far excellent companies such as Nordstrom will go to take proper care of their customers: "If Nordstrom can take back tires, shouldn't *you* rise to that level too?"

In a meeting about twenty years ago, I had the chance to ask Jim Nordstrom about the tire story. He smiled and said, "I don't know. I wasn't there." An excellent nonanswer.

But the story persists. I heard it recently during a session led by a member of the International Speakers Hall of Fame.

That's the thing about myths. Many are rooted in some truth, expanding as the story is handed from one person to the next. The fact that, ultimately, a myth may sound too fantastic yet still be uniformly accepted only happens when other stories about the "hero" are probably true and somewhat consistent. The tire story speaks to an ideal of superior, even unbelievably high, customer service. And there are many stories of Nordstrom delivering just that. My own family has had several such experiences.

For example, Kay was shopping for Kelly's school clothes several years ago. She found an outfit she liked at Nordstrom. Unfortunately, the one that fit Kelly was missing the belt. The salesperson assured Kay she would find the right-sized belt and contact her. The next day, Kay received a phone call from the salesperson. "Hi, Kay! It's my day off, but I was thinking about that belt. I stopped in a nearby Macy's and they have the exact same outfit. They are holding the belt for you, and you can pick it up anytime."

That's an amazing customer-service story.

Stories like that help us believe that the tire story might be true: "Hey, if *this* can happen, I guess *that* can happen too!"

The other thing about myths is how much people like to share them with friends and peers. I can safely say that when I do share Kay's belt story, whether in a speech or just in conversation, others inevitably want to share their own amazing Nordstrom customer-service story. And so the myth spreads.

Smart companies understand the power of myth. Oh, they might use another word for it, such as *brand*, but when managed correctly, it's still the same. You see, the essence of your brand is the big, specific promise you make to your customers. What promise can you make that resonates with your target audience? Nordstrom doesn't explicitly declare it offers world-class customer service in its advertising, but we all have come to expect it. Why? Because the company *implicitly* shows us through great stories, such as my wife's, and *mythical* stories, such as the returned tires. And not only do those smart companies develop strong myth/brands, but they help spread them too. Yes, even Nordstrom does that.

That's the thing about your myth/brand. You must manage it. You must carry it around with you at all times. You cannot for one second allow somebody else to take control of your story.

You must also look for available tools to anchor your branding myth in the mind of your target market and trigger the memory even later.

Great brands almost always have great myths attached, whether they're in the B2C market or B2B.

Your Innovation Strategy

The first McDonald's drive-through was created in 1975, near an Arizona military base, to serve soldiers who weren't permitted to get out of their cars while wearing fatigues. The manager of the Fort Huachuca McDonald's was befuddled by the loss of potential business, so he looked for an answer. While sitting at his bank's drive-through window, the solution hit him. If money could be passed through a window, so could food! The first fast-food, drive-through window was created. Nowadays, between 50 and 70 percent of all sales are through the drive-through.[8]

This is an example of what I call Stealing Genius™.

As I pointed out earlier, too many industries are guilty of practicing a strategic orthodoxy. Everybody looks alike, and everybody acts alike. And the main reason for this is people tend to look at *each other* for new ideas. As a result, most competition doesn't create innovation. It creates conformity.

And you don't want that, do you?

---

8   "Fast Food Statistics Concerning Drive Thrus in the Recent Years," November 17, 2013, http://www.fastfoodmenuprices.com/fast-food-statistics-concerning-drive-thrus-recent-years/.

But innovation is *hard*. How often have you pulled your team together for a "brainstorming" session? You ask everybody to bring his or her best new ideas for whatever challenge you might have. Let's say you want to develop a new marketing campaign. So you get the flip chart out and open it up for suggestions.

Silence.

Until someone pipes up and says, "Well, I saw ABC Widget Inc. do this promotion giving away baby ducks at a trade show in Detroit. I don't know if they made any sales, but they gave away a *lot* of baby ducks! Maybe we can do something like that."

And everybody chimes in, "That's a great idea! We can do it even *better* than ABC Widget Inc. did! We'll give everybody *two* ducks!"

No, no, no, no, no, no, no.

As a kid, I had the opportunity to spend a little time with W. Edwards Deming, one of history's leading management consultants. Wikipedia states, "Many in Japan credit Deming as the inspiration for what has become known as the Japanese post-war economic miracle of 1950 to 1960, when Japan rose from the ashes of war to start Japan on the road to becoming the second largest economy in the world through processes founded on the ideas Deming taught."[9]

One of the foundation blocks of Deming's approach to total-quality management was benchmarking. The definition I was taught was "to observe correct behavior and implement within your own context." Deming shared that companies often made a big mistake with benchmarking. Observing correct behavior within your industry only gives you a comparison of how you're doing. If you truly want to innovate you must put yourself *outside* your comfort zone, exposing yourself to alien experiences (my words). Observing correct behavior

---

9   "W. Edwards Deming," Wikipedia, https://en.wikipedia.org/wiki/W._Edwards_ Deming.

among aliens can often stimulate completely new ways of looking at something common in your world.

The Fort Huachuca McDonald's manager had most likely driven through his bank's drive-through many times. But when he had a need for a new solution, he was smart enough to look elsewhere, not just at other restaurants.

That's Stealing Genius™.

Your Experience Strategy

The commoditization of businesses today focuses on the three traditional components of competition:

- product

- price

- customer service

Technology has all but erased companies' abilities to create a product that differentiates them from the competition. Price cutting has never been a long-term success strategy. Oh, many have tried and many have dominated for short periods of time, but nobody has sustained. Even vaunted Walmart (home of the "Every Day Low Prices") has been soundly usurped by Amazon. Eventually, someone will take down Amazon too. Jeff Bezos has already predicted it.[10] Which leaves today's company to fend for itself on customer service. Because it's the last of the big three competition components to survive, it's the one most businesses look to.

Unfortunately, it hasn't been that easy. After all, what defines good-to-great customer service? Plus, there's a giant Achilles heel in providing great customer service: *people*. Businesses have to rely on

---

10   Charlie Rose, "Amazon's Jeff Bezos Looks to the Future," CBS News, December 1, 2013, http://www.cbsnews.com/news/amazons-jeff-bezos-looks-to-the-future/.

people to deliver world-class customer service, and apparently, it's just not that easy. At our local mall, a Nordstrom and a Macy's are located just a few hundred feet apart. From a customer-service perspective, they might as well be on different planets. If you walk into Macy's after passing through Nordstrom, you can actually *feel* the level of customer service drop. It's as if the temperature fell twenty degrees.

Certainly, you should work hard at educating your team to deliver the best customer service possible, but there is now a fourth component to add to the product/price/service list: your customer's experience.

Now granted, your customer's experience is immensely impacted by the customer service delivered. But it can go far beyond. You can develop a customer experience that, literally, creates an Uncopyable Attachment for your customer.

Just look at *Hamilton*. And Disney. And American Girl. And Harley-Davidson. All have created incredible experiences for their customers. And the following happen when you create incredible experiences for your customers:

- A richly imprinted experience wants to be repeated.

- A richly imprinted experience wants to be remembered.

- A richly imprinted experience wants to be shared.

As you progress through the rest of this book, look for those new perspectives and ideas that whack you upside the head just lightly. It might be in your branding strategy. It might be in your innovation strategy. It might be in your experience strategy. Heck, it might be in more than one!

Regardless, the point is you need to look for ways to get your customer *attached* to you, both professionally and personally. That's how you separate yourself from the competition.

BONUS CONTENT AND
WORKBOOK AVAILABLE AT
UNCOPYABLETHEBOOK.COM

CHAPTER TWO

The Marketing Diamond™

I'll bet you're actually using marketing backward. Yes, backward. The good news is I'm also betting every one of your competitors is marketing backward too.

Let me explain.

Let's imagine sales aren't where you'd like them to be. The graph is moving in the wrong direction—down—and you want to do something about it. You ask yourself what you can do. And the answer hits you: a mailing!

So you rent a list of five thousand people who fit your target market. You start thinking about what you can send those people. "Let's send our catalog!" a fellow staffer says.

"That would be too expensive," you reply. "Wait, I know. Let's print a two-sided flyer and mail that out. Wait, even better! We can make it a *self-mailer*. Print both sides but make it a trifold, so we can stick a label on and then mail it! Wait, wait! We can send them out using *bulk mail*! That'll save even *more* money!"

So you and your team create the trifold self-mailer, have it printed with bulk-mail indices in the corner, and stick on the mailing labels.

Someone takes them to the post office, and you all pat yourselves on the back for a job well done! Sales should start picking up again soon.

Then you take off your marketing hat. You go back to your office and resume work.

Then the mail arrives.

You pick up the stack of mail and stand over the trash can. You start flipping through the mail, quickly separating the "A" pile from the "B" pile. After tossing another piece into your "B" can, you notice a trifold self-mailer. It's got a mailing label with your name stuck on the front. In the corner is a bulk-mail stamp.

What do you do with that piece? You throw it straight into the trash can! It's junk mail.

You're no longer wearing the marketing hat—the hat you wear when you decide what to *send*. You're now receiving the marketing piece, and you have a very different perspective.

Another scenario: An advertising salesperson convinces you to make an appointment with her. She's selling packs of postcard coupons in a big mailer. "This goes out to forty-three thousand people, and you can have a postcard with your specific message inside for less than six cents per person!"

Wow, forty-three thousand people for less than six cents each? you think. *That's a great deal. Heck, if I only get a .01 percent response that's still FOUR new customers! That's worth it!*

Scenarios like this are countless. And each one of them is an example of marketing completely backward.

Choosing the medium *first*—a bulk-mail campaign, Val-Pak, a trade ad, social media, or any other tool—is doing it backward. Media does not drive your marketing. The first step in developing any marketing strategy starts with the market. Who are the prospects in your ideal target market?

In 1986 I was a guest on Robert Schuller's *Hour of Power*. Dr. Schuller was a televangelist based at the Crystal Cathedral in Garden Grove, California. His was a megachurch with seating for four thousand people. At the time, the *Hour of Power* TV program was broadcast worldwide to about thirteen million. It's not important why I was a guest, but that day was pivotal in my career. There were two services every Sunday and after the second, Dr. Schuller invited me back to his office for a cup of coffee.

"You were very good out there!" he said. "You should think about being a professional speaker!"

"Huh? A professional speaker? Get paid to speak? I had no idea you could do that."

He laughed, "Oh yes, you can get paid very well to speak to corporations and conferences!"

"But how do you find people to hire you?"

Now here I was, a marketing specialist, asking for marketing advice. I should have known better, but his answer was awesome.

"Well, how do you hunt moose?"

"Huh?" I said again. I was definitely caught off-guard.

Dr. Schuller laughed and went on. "Well, you wouldn't go to Florida to hunt moose would you? No! You'd go farther north, maybe into Canada. You'd look for a forest where moose lived—where a *lot* of moose lived. And would you attract moose with Hostess Ding Dongs? No! You'd use some kind of moose bait, something moose would love to get and none of the other animals cared about. And would you capture a moose with a tennis racquet? No! You'd need some sort of moose gun—a big gun that's especially made for an animal the size of a moose.

"But the most important thing to understand is you're hunting moose! That's first. There are a lot of animals in the forest—bears, wild turkeys, otters, maybe big cats, birds, and fish in the streams—but you aren't interested in any of those other animals. You are only interested in moose."

I've carried that marketing lesson ever since, and it makes for the strategic-marketing foundation for all of my clients and for developing an *Uncopyable Attachment* for their customers.

Over the years, I've refined how I look at the advice Dr. Schuller gave me and developed a simple model. I call it the Marketing Diamond.

The Marketing Diamond starts at the top and works counterclockwise.

MARKET

The first step in any strategy is to define and understand your market. That's the top of the diamond. And as Dr. Schuller explained, it's the most critical.

Look at it this way: If your objective is to establish an Uncopyable Attachment with your customers, should your primary efforts be in deciding which media to use, or understanding exactly who your target prospects are along with their needs, challenges, and aspirations?

Who is your market? Who is your moose? How narrowly can you define your market? What do you know about your market? What keeps your market prospects awake at night? What problems, challenges, obstacles, aspirations, objectives, and projects do they have? The more clearly you can define your market (your moose), the better.

I remember sitting in a meeting of Nordstrom executives, a few years after my meeting with Dr. Schuller. Jim Nordstrom called me in to add an outside voice in their meeting. Every time an idea came out, someone at the table would ask, "Well, how do you think Barbara would feel about this?" And they'd talk about Barbara. Another idea was suggested, and once again, someone asked what Barbara would think.

I was confused. I began wondering why, if Barbara was so important, wasn't *she* at this meeting?

They all laughed and said, "Barbara isn't real. She's our ideal customer. She's forty years old, married with two kids, has a household income of $150,000, is fairly social, and upwardly mobile. Whenever we make a decision, we try to put ourselves in Barbara's head and wonder what she would think."

They were hunting moose! And it was my first real exposure to a common practice now known as developing your avatar. If you can create a mental picture of your ideal customer, it makes it much easier to think like your customer.

An important distinction to make here is the difference between a prospect and a lead.

When you identify the demographics and characteristics of your market, you are defining how they *fit* with you. Most companies have no problem describing their specific Barbara, as Nordstrom did. When you do that, you are describing a *prospect*. A prospect fits the profile of your target market. But there's a second and very critical behavior prospects must display in order to be labeled *leads*.

They must show some level of *interest*.

For example, let's say I'm a new car salesperson. If I were to look at you, there's a good chance you would fit the profile of my target, my moose. I think you *need* to buy a new car.

But do *you* think you need a new car? Maybe you do. Maybe you don't. If you do, you might be willing to meet me at the dealership and test drive a couple of cars. But if you *don't* think you need a new car, what are the odds of my selling you one? Slim to none, probably.

That's where *level of interest* comes in. If you fit the profile I've defined and you display some level of interest, then you now change from a prospect into a lead. The better you fit my profile and the higher your level of interest, the more highly qualified you are and the more likely it is you're going to buy from me.

I can find lists of prospects via list brokers. I can find prospects in groups and forums online. I can find prospects reading an industry trade magazine. But I'm only going to use those media to *uncover the leads among those prospects*. I'm going to send communications to my moose, my prospects, to get a percentage of them to raise their hands and say, "I'm interested in what you're saying. Please stay in touch with me." That's the moose you want to attract.

MESSAGE

The second point on the Marketing Diamond is your message. Does your message match the market?

This is where you develop your bait, the bait that gets the moose's attention and attracts him to you. Just as important, your message, or bait, does *not* attract all the other animals in the forest. Think of a dog whistle as a good example of the perfect message. You blow a dog whistle and you get the attention of dogs. Only dogs can hear it. It's sending the perfect message.

The message is always delivered from the market's perspective, not yours. Remember, the market *wants* to hear your message.

Robert Collier was an early marketing/advertising pioneer and author of *The Robert Collier Letter Book*. (I highly recommend this book for those who are interested in writing better copy.) He wrote:

> *You know that every man is constantly holding a mental conversation with himself, the burden of which is his own interests—his business, his loved ones, his advancement. And you have tried to chime in on that conversation with something that fits with his thoughts.*

Another way to interpret Collier's message is to *always enter the* conversation *that is already taking place in the* customer's mind.

The better we are at understanding what our market is thinking, the easier it will be to develop a relationship.

What keeps your market prospects awake at night? What's the first thing on their mind when they wake up? What challenges, problems, and hurdles are they facing? On the flip side, what are their aspirations, dreams, and goals? Think about it this way: If you're young and single, you probably aren't thinking about life insurance. But when you get married and have a baby, you might start worrying about your family's future if something were to happen to you. That's the perfect time for an insurance salesperson to get your attention.

The better the job you do in matching a message to your market, the more successful you'll be.

Now imagine you come up with a message only you can say, only you can promise, only you can deliver. That's where the concept of Uncopyable comes in.

Messages come in all shapes and forms. A message can be delivered in your branding proposition. It can be delivered in a trade ad. It can be something shared in social media. It can be in a white paper, or a webinar, or an event. A message can be delivered in many different ways.

MEDIA

The third point of the Marketing Diamond is media. Now we can start thinking about the tool we should use to communicate with our market. We're now looking for the most effective and efficient means of communicating with our moose. We want to *go* to our moose.

Do our market prospects attend a trade show? Then I'm exhibiting at that show. Do they read certain magazines? Then I'm looking to advertise or get an article published. Are they on social media? Maybe I can target them with Facebook's Audience Insights. Even better, our market may be in a group.

The point is to look where you can effectively and efficiently reach your prospects *after* you've identified them and developed your message. It's just plain dumb to pick a medium first and then hope your market is there.

There are hundreds of possible tools you can use to reach prospects. And here's something very important to remember: they *all* work for somebody! Anybody who tells you to put all of your marketing dollars into one tool (SEO, social media, anybody?) is simply trying to sell that tool to you. Period. I recently encouraged a corporate client to provide fax-back forms in addition to an online URL in a direct-mail campaign. The client reluctantly agreed and was shocked by how many people used the fax. I studied the prospective moose and figured it still had a fax machine sitting next to its desk—and I was right.

MOMENT

The fourth point on my Marketing Diamond sits on the right side: the moment. I believe the purpose of marketing is to be on the mind of exactly the right prospect when the prospect is ready to buy. We don't know when that moment will be and, too often, our marketing efforts are really aimed only at people who are ready to buy *right now.*

But unless you have a low-cost, impulse item, the majority of prospects will not be ready to buy from you right now. When we are communicating with our market, we should always be cognizant of this. Think about developing your relationship for this reason: When the lightning bolt comes out of the sky and strikes your prospects on the head, causing them to say, "I need that product right now!" do they think of you first? Do they think of you second? Do they think of you at all?

The objective of an Uncopyable marketer is to be the *only* source your prospects think about.

Something else to consider regarding moment is to ask yourself whether you can *make the prospect feel uncomfortable or even pain.* People will change an opinion or behavior when they become dissatisfied, so can you *make* them dissatisfied?

Developing the Marketing Diamond for your company takes time. But once in place, that plan literally becomes a system for you—a flywheel, if you will. You can flip the switch anytime and prospects become leads, ultimately becoming customers.

If you'd like to download a worksheet taking you through the Marketing Diamond, you can get it free at uncopyablethebook.com/diamond.

IN A NUTSHELL

Step 1: Define your market.

Who are your market prospects? What profile can you define that covers them? Are they in a specific geographic location? Maybe you specialize in working with companies of a certain size, in terms of annual revenues, or number of employees. What are the titles of your prospects? Are they the owner or CEO? Maybe they're a production engineer or a web designer. The more clearly you can define your moose, the more you can laser-beam your messaging to it.

Step 2: What message resonates with your market?

The bigger the problem you solve for your customers or clients, the more valuable you are to them. What pain point do they have that you can remove? If you can identify that pain, you'll win. People will move heaven and earth to get rid of pain.

Step 3: What media are most effective and efficient?

Where can you communicate with a lot of your prospects? Do they hang out on Facebook or in LinkedIn groups? Maybe there's an online forum for just them. Auto Shop Owner, for example, is an online forum for several thousand automotive after-market repair shops.

Step 4: When will your moose be ready to buy?

When is that buy moment? Some industries have naturally long lead times; others not so much. Nevertheless, planning your communication strategy around the typical lead time helps keep you on the mind of the prospect when the prospect is ready to buy.

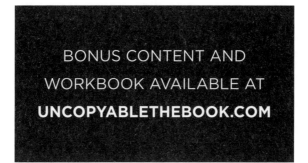

TWO
TWO
TWO

THE THREE UNCOPYABLE STRATEGIES

CHAPTER THREE

Uncopyable Branding

What makes you Uncopyable—so Uncopyable your moose will come running out of the woods to find you? We've already established what it's *not:* it's not your price, your product, or your stellar customer service.

It's your branding proposition: your big promise. Your branding proposition goes beyond simply uniquely identifying your products and services. It makes a clearly stated promise as to how you differentiate yourself from the competition, one that resonates powerfully with your moose. But *branding* is a muddy word with as many definitions as *customer service,* so let's begin by getting clear on the concept.

Sometimes, people fall into the trap of thinking marketing should be all about creating brand awareness, but what does that mean? You can't really measure it, and it's not worth much unless you're also creating persuasion. Brand awareness without persuasion is like getting a prescription before a diagnosis from a doctor. That's corporate malpractice.

When you think of branding, the first thing that comes to mind is probably a logo, the thing corporations like to slap up on their buildings, their websites, their can coolers, or whatever they pass out. You might think effective branding is mostly about stamping your logo on everything that doesn't move. And that's about as far as most people get with it.

But your branding proposition goes beyond uniquely identifying your products and services. It not only makes a clearly stated promise; it also makes you memorable to your moose.

Some years back, I was consulting for a client in Milwaukee. We finished up one morning and headed out to go golfing. Milwaukee has three freeways that divide up the city. One goes north-south, and two of them run parallel, east-west. The golf course where we were playing was, literally, at the intersection where an east-west freeway bisected the north-south freeway. As we played, I heard this low rumble off in the distance. Now, the weather was fabulous—not a cloud in the sky—so I asked the guy, "Do you have any idea what that sound is?"

And he said, "Oh, yeah. It's probably the Harleys coming to town."

Every five years, Harley-Davidson owners from all corners of the USA start driving toward Milwaukee. They form a kind of parade as they all head for the fairgrounds, which was the noise I was hearing: a hundred thousand Harley-Davidson motorcycles thundering by us on the freeway. We could see them—lots of black leather, bandannas, vests—and everything was stamped with the Harley logo.

I said to my client, "Gee, I better get back to my hotel after we're done, lock the door, and order room service to protect myself from these guys." I was half joking, but sure enough, I went downtown, got into my hotel room, turned the TV on, and the big story on the local news was about the Harley festival. This young reporter was interviewing one of the executives from Harley-Davidson: "What are you doing to provide security to keep the city safe while all of these thousands and thousands of Harley owners are in town?"

The executive laughed and said, "What you don't understand is what we sell is the ability for a forty-three-year-old accountant to dress in black leather, ride through small towns, and have people be afraid of them."

I could not write that down fast enough when he said it because it was like a light going on. I mean I've got a lot of friends who have Harleys, and I guarantee you, they're exactly what he described—and you know who you are!

That's the Harley-Davidson branding promise: no matter what your day job is, when you come rolling into town on your Harley, dressed in your black leather logo jacket, with all the other accountants and dentists on their Harleys roaring alongside you, you will be magically transformed into bad-asses, and you'll be part of a community.

Harley-Davison does not sell motorcycles.

It sells fantasy and community, a branding proposition that's uniquely Harley and difficult for other companies to copy.

Now, imagine if Harley's branding proposition were that "we sell the highest quality of motorcycles, backed by the best customer service, giving the average person an enjoyable and thrilling ride." That's, typically, the type of statement companies make about themselves. Not exactly a call to the wild side, is it?

There are people who have no interest in getting on a bike and riding around with a whole bunch of other people. They don't care about community. They don't care about sound or black leather jackets. Those people will never buy a Harley—*and Harley doesn't care, because they're not Harley's moose.*

Why is it so important to differentiate yourself and to create a branding proposition you can deliver on?

Branding clearly *differentiates you* from the competition.

Branding *establishes your credibility* with your marketplace.

Branding *resonates* with your moose.

Branding *makes a unique promise.*

Branding *makes you the logical choice* for your target market.

Branding *makes you memorable.*

And—important for your moose—branding *removes risk.*

Best of all, you don't have to be a big name like Harley-Davidson to come up with a compelling brand proposition.

My client Stor-Loc makes those high-end toolboxes and tool cabinets like the ones you see at the service bay of a car dealership. They're for people who have a lot of tools and who need a really well-made cabinet in which to store them. When I started working with that company, its quasi-branding proposition was, "Think outside the box," not exactly an unfamiliar phrase, and the response to that was generally along the lines of "Yawn."

I told these guys, "Look. We need to come up with some type of branding proposition you can tell the people you want to sell to that will immediately make them say, 'Oh, yeah. *That's* what I'm looking for.'"

We ended up with this promise: "This is the best toolbox you'll ever buy, and it's 100 percent guaranteed for fifty-five years." The tagalong line was "It's 100 percent made in the USA in every way." Now, when people who are looking for a professional-quality toolbox hear that, they know this isn't a cheap piece of junk but something they'll be able to hand over to their kids.

No questions asked, nothing whatsoever, just a rock-solid 100 percent guarantee. Not everyone would have the nerve to say that, but Mike Ryan, the owner of Stor-Loc, jumped on it. Now add the odd-sounding but dramatic fifty-five-year life of the guarantee, and you've got a memorable, Uncopyable game changer.

That's the kind of branding proposition that helps you to create a monopoly in the mind of the customer or prospect with a big promise that would be difficult for the competition to steal. I mean, what can they do? Offer fifty-six years? It's sticky: their customers remember that fifty-five-year promise—and it resonates.

DON'T JUST THINK OUTSIDE THE BOX—BUILD YOUR OWN BOX

Think about your brain as having a nearly infinite warehouse of memories, perceptions, opinions, and viewpoints. There's a little guy in charge of your warehouse.

If I say the word *motorcycle*, that little guy goes running to find the box labeled "motorcycle"—the box that has everything you ever learned, thought about, read about, talked about, related to the word *motorcycle* in it—and he brings it out front. For some people, the word in their box is *dangerous*: motorcycles kill people; people who ride them are criminals—stuff like that. In someone else's box, *motorcycle* means freedom, hit the road, feel the wind in your hair, and get bugs in your teeth.

For many of us, even names such as Kawasaki, Yamaha, Honda, or Suzuki would all be in that same box. Why? Because the messages and experiences we've received from those manufacturers, over the years, are all pretty much the same. And if those manufacturers are all in the same box, how do they get our attention? By shouting louder than the competition. I call it playground shouting.

The idea of creating an effective branding proposition is that it's *not* that you're trying to think outside the box; you're trying to create your *own* box, one that's completely separate from the others.

Harley-Davidson has done a great job of building its own box, filling it with its own stuff and hammering its uniqueness home to the marketplace. Remember Harley-Davidson sells fantasy and community. Its bikes are built for the road, not the racetrack. It fills its box with messaging and "souvenirs" to reinforce that branding proposition. Besides all the black leather jackets, how many companies do you know of whose customers tattoo their brand on their body? I have yet to see a Vespa tramp stamp.

That's what *you* want to do: build your own box and fill it with the things that will resonate with your moose, things that keep you out of that big generic box your competitors are all in.

To do that, you've got to look at what makes you unique—and work it.

WHAT MAKES YOU SO SPECIAL? IF YOU DON'T KNOW, NEITHER WILL ANYONE ELSE

Sometimes, companies have a hard time coming up with their unique branding proposition. Stor-Loc, for example, didn't have a unique personality. But the guarantee of fifty-five years and 100 percent made in the USA spelled out what the company is: dependable, rock solid. No, it's not a wholly fresh idea, but the company laid it out there strongly and added that touch of appealing quirkiness with the fifty-five-year guarantee.

There are companies whose founder, if not the company itself, has a unique personality. Certainly, compared to most consultants, I have a unique personality and a good measure of quirkiness. I come with an edge. One client mentioned over dinner, "You should come with a disclaimer." I love that!

If your promise isn't all that unique, maybe your personality is. When you're looking to break out of the scrum of sameness, trying to determine a brand or a branding proposition, you might come up with a promise and use that personality to make it stick—and stick out.

Smart companies play up what sets them apart.

You think it bothered Frank Perdue that people made cracks about him looking a lot like one of the chickens he sold? Hardly. In fact, he embraced it and even used it in his TV commercials. He was a genius at branding. One of my favorites among his sayings is "if you can differentiate a dead chicken, you can differentiate anything."

This can be a tough proposition for buttoned-up types. Even brave guys get timid when you urge them to step out of the lineup and get a little goofy. I worked with a company where the owner had great bantering humor, but he absolutely didn't want that to be a part of the company's branding. That was a lost opportunity, and too many companies take themselves too seriously.

Not Southwest Airlines founder Herb Kelleher. He had an outsized, "out-there" personality, and he loved doing big promotional stunts—the goofier the better. Once, when another company threatened to sue the airline for a copyright infringement because it used the phrase "Just Plane Smart" in its advertising, Kelleher challenged the owner of that other small business to an arm-wrestling match. He proposed they put up a substantial amount of money to go to the winner's choice of charities, and the winner also would get the right to the slogan. Mind you, Kelleher was in his sixties at the time, and the other guy was in his thirties and athletic, so Kelleher had no chance to beat this guy, but the publicity this idea generated was great for both of them. They had this quasi-wrestling match dubbed "Malice in Dallas" in front of a whole bunch of people, and they declared it a tie, agreeing both could use the slogan and the money would go to the Muscular Dystrophy Association and Ronald McDonald House of Cleveland.[11]

The success and fame that a handful of regional businesses created for themselves by daring to go big with their personalities speaks for how well this tactic can work. Think of Cal Worthington, the legendary car dealer, or Frank Carvel, the ice-cream cake manufacturer with the gravelly voice, who did his own very memorable commercials.

If there's something special about your office culture, use it. Do you love hunting so much you shut your business down periodically to take everyone hunting? Go with a camo theme as your color, and talk about your hunting trips. If your owner has a funny way of

---

11   The Build Network staff, "3 Lasting Lessons from Malice in Dallas," *Inc.*, July 22, 2013, accessed November 1, 2016, http://www.inc.com/3-lasting-lessons-from-malice-in-dallas.html.

expressing himself or an outsized personality, put it out there and make him a star because that's Uncopyable.

And that's what you want to be.

THE UNCOPYABLE BOX

Five branding tools for building *your* unique box:

1. Own a Word or Phrase.

Take ownership of a word or a phrase, something that connects to your promise. A famous example is Volvo. When people are thinking about buying a new car, if their primary concern is "I've got to protect the kids," they're automatically going to think of Volvo because Volvo owns the word *safety*, and it would be difficult or impossible for another company to steal that word from them. Another example is Disney World, which is known as "The Happiest Place on Earth"— not "happy" or "happier" but "happiest." With Amazon, the word is *responsive*. If you're a Prime member and you order something— *boom*—it's there. For Ben and Jerry's, the word is *quirky*, and whatever they put out there has to reflect that quirkiness.

Stuck for a word that resonates for you and your brand? Try these:

dependable	problem solver
overdeliver	responsive
fun	conscientious
friendly	thorough
sophisticated	unique
experienced	knowledgeable
trustworthy	partner
diligent	personalized
specialist	

(For a longer list, go to uncopyablethebook.com/words.)

You could look at any one of those, and say, "That word resonates with us, so we're going to take that word now. How do we reinforce it? How can we symbolize it? How do we get into the minds of customers and prospects so they connect that word with us?"

Words and phrases are part of my branding. "I'm Kelly's Dad," and "I'm the Marketing Gunslinger" are in my box too, and when others try to purloin these ideas (e.g., "I'm John's dad"), I've actually had clients say to them, "You're copying Miller," and shut them down.

Small businesses are in a better place to do this than big businesses because small businesses are, typically, working with a smaller group of moose, a smaller group of competitors. They're not competing against the megacompanies. That makes it much easier for small businesses to take ownership of a word or phrase and make it part of the branding messaging. If you're not doing this, you should be.

2. Own a Color.

A twist on the word strategy, and one small companies don't use often enough, is to pick a color and own it. Coca-Cola owns red. Starbucks owns green. IBM owns blue—but you don't have to be a multinational to own a color.

In my world, I own the color orange. When I speak in public, I'm always wearing an orange shirt or sweater. My phone case is orange. My reading glasses are orange. When I send gifts to people, 100 percent of the time those gifts are orange. And when I mail things to people, they are in orange envelopes. My word, as you've probably guessed, is Uncopyable, so I connect Uncopyable with orange. I tell people, "Whenever you see orange, think of the word Uncopyable." What that creates is both an anchor and a trigger because it anchors in your mind the word Uncopyable, and that makes you think of Steve Miller.

Does it work? People tell me all the time, "I can't see the color orange without thinking about you and Uncopyable." Orange has become so strongly associated with me I've gone to board meetings where every person in the room was wearing an orange shirt because they connect me with orange, and then they connect me with Uncopyable. So nobody, nobody, can take that from me; no other consultant or speaker or anybody playing in my sandbox can commandeer orange without getting chastised by the marketplace.

3. Create Triggers and Anchors.

Consider all the different types of tools you could use to *anchor* your promise in the mind of the customer or prospect and *trigger* the memory of your name.

Souvenirs, advertising specialties, have been around for a very long time. There's nothing wrong with using them as long as you are a lot more creative than most people are. But they're not the only way to go.

Perfect example: A number of years ago, the luxury-pen manufacturer Mont Blanc came out with a series called The Generation. These pens came in six different colors, and one of them was called adventure orange. They were not cheap, and I gave one to each of my best clients. Since then, Mont Blanc has discontinued the line, and these pens have become collectors' pieces worth a lot of money.

But you know what's worth money to me? When I'm in clients' offices, every one of those high-value clients is using an orange Mont Blanc. And I know it's not unusual for people to see that beautiful pen and ask my clients where they got it.

You can do things that touch one or a few people, or you can do things that touch a whole bunch of people. The important thing is to keep your tactic congruent with your message and your branding proposition and to not just use some generic, could-be-anyone's thing.

I found these very cool, orange, dog whistles and have been giving them out to my audiences and clients. Naturally, I changed the labels on them to read, "Moose Whistle," and I tell my listeners, "Okay. When you blow this whistle, only moose can hear it. If we were out in the forests of northern America, in the northern USA, or in Canada, and we were to blow these whistles, we'd get stampeded by moose because they're the perfect moose bait. Hang yours on your computer or somewhere you're going to see it every single day to remind you to use bait your moose can't resist."

The message has to match the market. This whistle is an anchor when I give it to clients, and when it's hung where they can see it every day, it becomes a trigger that reminds them of my message—and me!

I've got a client who decided to own the color red and couple it with the word *specialists*. The company is using this combination at trade shows, in mailings, in the logo—everywhere. And it's working because it's sticky.

4. Create Your Own Language.

Seriously. The great example of this, of course, is Starbucks. Nobody knew how to order coffee until Starbucks taught us how: the Venti, half-caf, triple-skinny, extra-hot, caramel latte may have existed somewhere in the universe before Starbucks invented it, but we didn't know how to order it. Now, all those who are Starbucks regulars can rattle this stuff off as if they were born speaking fluent Coffee.

Disney doesn't have "customers"; it has "guests." It doesn't have "employees" either; it's got "cast members" to remind Disney employees they are onstage at all times and that no matter how lowly their job may be, they're essential to creating the Disney experience and need to act the part. The Ritz-Carlton tells both customers and staff that "we are ladies and gentlemen, serving ladies and gentlemen."

I have my own language, and I'm pretty strict about how it gets used. When the *Wall Street Journal* interviewed me, a few years ago, they balked when I told them my title is Kelly's Dad and Marketing Gunslinger. They felt that wasn't professional enough for them. I said, "You want to put me in a big box with all the other speakers and consultants. I have my own box and my title is Kelly's Dad, Marketing Gunslinger." They've now used it several times. Apparently, they haven't lost any subscribers.

I don't have fans, friends, followers, or subscribers. I have BFFs. Everybody's a BFF. And since I've been using that phrase for a while, when people contact me, they'll say something like "I've been a BFF for two years," which tells me they're speaking my language.

Once you create that language, it's yours. And everyone you interact with will associate those words and phrases with you alone.

5. Shock and Awe.

When you identify and contact a whale, what do you send? Your printed catalog that's sent to anybody who can fog a mirror? A warm-form letter saying something like, "Dear Mr. Smith, it was a great pleasure talking with you today. Enclosed herewith please find our annual 10-K, a catalog of the rest of our line we didn't talk about today, and a price list of our entire line of products and services." Yawn.

When you get new customers, what do you send them? A copy of the agreement? An invoice for the first payment? An arrogant e-mail that reads, "Congratulations on your decision to work with us!"

No. No. And no!

Uncopyable marketers use this early-in-the-relationship opportunity to reinforce and enhance the new relationship and offer more evidence separating them from the competition.

Soon after I signed the agreement to publish this book with Advantage Media, I received a big blue box weighing five pounds. Here's what was inside:

- a handwritten welcome-to-the-team note from my contact, Keith Kopcsak

- three books about how to be a successful author, how to sell more books, and brainstorming

- a collection of six CDs from other Advantage Media Group authors titled *Author Success University*

- a giant poster with an infographic about book publishing

- a microwave package of Orville Redenbacher popcorn

This is known as a shock-and-awe package.

Early in my speaking career and well before the Internet, I used shock and awe to generate new speaking dates, although I didn't know it was called that. Mine wasn't nearly as nice as Advantage's. When I got a good prospect, I'd fill a box with copies of all the testimonial letters I'd collected. There were a *lot*. I'd include videos of me speaking and, usually, an unusual gift—a pair of orange sunglasses, an orange "moose" whistle, or something else. I'd include copies of every article I'd ever written or been interviewed for and, of course, copies of all my books.

My objective was to overwhelm my prospect with a preponderance of proof that I was the right guy for the job. And it worked.

What type of shock-and-awe package can you produce to send to prospects, to new customers? By putting in the effort to truly wow your market, I guarantee you will stand far apart from the competition.

So where do you get ideas like the ones I just shared? That's another arrow Uncopyable marketers have in their quiver. It's a powerful technique I call Stealing Genius, and it gets its own chapter. Read on.

BONUS CONTENT AND
WORKBOOK AVAILABLE AT
UNCOPYABLETHEBOOK.COM

CHAPTER FOUR

Uncopyable Innovation: Stealing Genius™

These days when you get into your car and you want to listen to music, you wirelessly connect your smart phone via Bluetooth to your car's sound system and rock Spotify. But it wasn't always like that, kids.

First, there was this thing called radio. You turned it on and hoped it would play something you wanted to hear. Most of the time, you just took what you got because the alternative was silence.

Then someone got the bright idea of giving people a way to play their music in their cars. Getting from there to here was a bumpy ride. Back in this benighted time, Chrysler actually came out with a car with a turntable built into it, one that popped down from under the dash and played 45s. If you think about the needle skipping along with every bump and swerve, you can see why that didn't catch on. But the concept of having your music when you wanted it was a good one. It just needed better technology.

Bill Lear, who was an engineer at Motorola and the founder of LearJet, was a man of incredible invention. He never stopped having ideas. One of the things he put thought into was this notion of portable music. There was a fairly new product on the market called the 4-track, and he, initially, got involved with it. It was a really clunky mechanism that involved using tape instead of record players, which was clearly a step in the right direction. He went out looking for somebody who could help him build this new audio product.

He found my dad.

My dad had made a name for himself as a top-flight audio engineer and product developer in the audio and video world. So he brought my dad in, and together, they came up with the first working 8-track tape player.

It changed music for everybody. It changed it for audiences. It changed it for the industry, for rock bands, and for radio. It changed it for teens, who could now cue up their favorite make-out music. People were now free to carry their own music with them, not only in their cars but on portable players too.

During the time they were developing this product, Dad and Lear were trying to figure out where they were going to manufacture it. Most of the money Lear had raised was going into jets, so there wasn't much left over to build 8-tracks. They were originally based in Detroit and tried to produce them there, but labor costs were too high. They tried to start up a facility near their offices in Tucson, Arizona. The labor was cheap, but local officials were expensive.

It was my dad who came up with the idea of building it in Japan. If you remember back that far, in the 1960s, "Made in Japan" had a very different connotation from what it has today. "Made in Japan" meant the product was junk. Japan was still in the midst of rebuilding after World War II, and the only quality products coming out of Japan at that time were those little colored umbrellas you stick in drinks. But labor costs were attractively rock bottom, and my dad saw the opportunity there. All they'd have to do was to figure out a way to build quality into the product.

So they brought in an American who was already in Japan, consulting for a lot of companies. His name was W. Edwards Deming.

Deming had revolutionized Toyota, which bought big into Deming's philosophy of total-quality management, meaning, essentially, that quality is built in *before* the product gets made. In the past, there'd been this notion of quality control, in which products were tested as they rolled off the production line. If they didn't work, they were rejected. Deming realized that was costing money, and he was very successful in creating a corporate culture built around doing it right.

As a young teenager, I was dragged on trips for some father-son time. Sometimes, we traveled with Lear and/or Deming. Both were brilliant guys. Lear was great to hang with; Deming . . . not so much. He was a bit irascible and not really fond of hanging out with kids.

I picked up, from listening to him, one thing in particular that kind of stuck in my head, and many years later, it popped up again: his concept of benchmarking, which is one of the cornerstones of total-quality management. What Deming used to describe as the key idea of benchmarking was studying other companies. You studied other organizations. You examined what they were very, very good at, and you took that knowledge back to your company and emulated it within your own context.

Deming said there are two broad definitions of benchmarking: internal benchmarking and external benchmarking, or intrinsic and extrinsic benchmarking. Essentially, internal benchmarking means you benchmark your own industry. You study what your competition is doing because you need to know where you stand relative to your competitors.

While, of course, you do have to be aware of what the competition is up to, Deming felt the problem with internal benchmarking is that you never get new ideas from your competition. You can only take their improvements and maybe make them a little better.

This goes back to what we've talked about before. Industries follow this strategic orthodoxy in which companies look at each other, within their industry, and they all copy each other. And when they copy each other, what happens? Eventually, nobody's different in any meaningful way. Competition breeds conformity, not innovation.

Deming said that was fine, as far as it went. His idea was that you use internal benchmarking for fuel, not for ideas. Yes, it would help keep you moving, but it couldn't be the end-all.

His groundbreaking idea was extrinsic benchmarking, *studying aliens*: you study people and organizations and businesses that have no relationship to your world at all. It sounds crazy. Why in the world would you do that? But here's an illustration.

One of my clients is CONEXPO, which is the largest tradeshow in the United States. It's in the construction industry, and it's enormous. I took the heads of CONEXPO to one of my Stealing Genius laboratories. On these special field trips, we explore other industries and look for ways to apply what they're doing to what we do. As part of this particular laboratory of going out and studying aliens, I told my clients we were going to visit the American Girl store in Chicago. I actually waited until we were, literally, on the bus before springing that news on them because I knew what the response was going to be from the male participants. I really wish I'd taken pictures of their faces when I announced our destination.

"I'm taking you to a doll store."

"We're going to a *what*?" (*Why are we paying you?*)

By the time we left the American Girl store, their jaws were on the floor because the ideas the trip had sparked for them were so many and so broad.

I don't know if you're familiar with American Girl, but you need to be. This was the original American Girl store. At the time, they had about eight dolls in their line, and each one represented a fictionalized girl's life at a different period in American history. For instance, my daughter's doll was Felicity, whose backstory was built around the era of the American Revolution. Everything that came with the doll—the clothes, accessories, and storybook about her life—was detailed and accurate in terms of the history represented.

At this particular store, they had, for each of these dolls, an actual museum-style case in which there were pictures and genuine artifacts from that doll's historic era, with explanations of what they were and how they'd have been used.

And CONEXPO stole that ingenious idea.

I remember, when I walked into their next trade show, they said, "Hey, Steve, come here and take a look at this."

They'd actually created a mini-museum right there at the show, a historical museum of the history of construction. Just as the American Girl store had done, they had different "windows" looking into the different eras of construction, complete with artifacts and pictures. It was fantastic.

I said, "Oh, wow! You took that from the American Girl store!"

They were all laughing; "Yeah, that's right, but just don't tell any of the other guys here."

Probably, the original stolen genius idea was the printing press. Yes, Gutenberg invented it, but he got the idea from seeing how wine presses were used to squeeze grape juice. His idea was to apply that to setting type and making impressions on paper. Pure stolen genius.

One of my favorite examples comes from back in the early days of Southwest Airlines's life. Looking at costs versus profit, one of the things the CEO Herb Kelleher realized was the airline did not make money when airplanes were on the ground. It only made money when airplanes were flying because people pay to fly. It takes most airlines at least forty-five minutes to an hour to clean up and prep a plane for new passengers between flights. How could he cut the downtime the planes spent on the ground?

He found the answer *from studying NASCAR pit crews.* During a race, every second spent getting more gas, a change of tires, or fixing a problem costs precious time on the track. Pit crews spend hundreds of hours practicing to get their job done and the car out as fast as possible.[12] Nowadays, Southwest has its planes loaded and ready to roll in about twenty minutes. They average 10.5 daily flights per gate, compared to the industry average of 5.0.[13]

How do they do it? Everyone pitches in—even the pilots—when it comes to cleaning and getting people on.[14]

Ever see a NASCAR pit crew in action? It's like a well-oiled machine: Everyone is in motion, doing what needs to be done, without a wasted move. If your car is in the pit, you're losing valuable distance on the track, so every millisecond counts. Herb Kelleher realized that kind of organized effort could solve his turnaround problem, so he hired a NASCAR pit crew to come in and teach his

---

12   Zack Albert, "Evolution of the Nascar Pit Stop: How Far It's Come," NASCAR, July 16, 2014, http://www.nascar.com/en_us/news-media/articles/2014/7/16/evolution-of-the-nascar-pit-stop-nascar-hall-of-fame.html.

13   Kevin Freiberg and Jackie Freiberg, *Nuts! Southwest Airlines' Crazy Recipe for Business and Personal Success* (New York: Crown Business, 1998).

14   Andrada Ghețe, "Southwest Airlines: from benchmarking to benchmarked," *Performance Magazine*, October 2, 2014, http://www.performancemagazine.org/southwest-airlines-from-benchmarking-to-benchmarked/.

people how to make every second count. That's one of the big reasons why Southwest Airlines is one of the top-grossing airlines around.

I took clients from Delphi Automotive, a big company out of Detroit, on a very casual Stealing Genius laboratory excursion. They were looking for some fresh ideas they could take to a major after-market trade show. We hit the mall to walk through the Apple store. With the Stealing Genius concept in mind, they started thinking about how Apple stores stood out from other computer and electronics retailers not only by virtue of their unique design but also by virtue of how people interacted with the merchandise, how they were greeted—the whole deal.

They went back and threw away all the old designs for their traditional tradeshow exhibits. They designed a booth that was very similar to the Apple store in its layout and in the experience, the interaction, and the engagement people would have with the staffers. *And nobody knew.* None of the visitors to the booth could tell that this was genius stolen from the Apple store, but, of course, everybody from Delphi knew that's where it came from. And it was a tremendously successful event.

Peter Drucker, who's generally acknowledged to be the godfather of modern corporate management, used to say there were only two things a corporation needed to do really, really well. One was marketing, and the other was innovation, and everything else played a support role to those two, including manufacturing and production.

So, from a marketing perspective, when you think about the concept of Uncopyable and start to talk about it in terms of branding and marketing, where do you come up with innovation? If you want to separate yourself from the crowd, innovation is what you're trying to do, but it's really hard to just innovate.

71

You call the staff together for a brainstorming session, and you've got a blank flip chart up front. Once everybody's seated, you say, "Okay. We need to come up with some new ideas on how to market our products," or "how to make ourselves seem better," or "how to do better customer service. Come on. Let's come up with some ideas. Let's brainstorm." Everybody sits there and just looks at each other with blank looks on their faces. And then, eventually, somebody says, "Well, you know, our competitor, ABC Company, I saw them do this." Everybody goes, "Yeah, yeah, we can do that. We can do it better than them!"

We mistake that for innovation, and of course, it's not. Improvement is what it is. *Improvement is not innovation.* Innovation is closer to game changing than it is to incremental upward movement.

Deming's philosophy came back to me years later. I used to play golf with Jim Nordstrom, who, at the time, was president of Nordstrom. When he got to know me, he said, "Hey, I think we want to hire you to come in and work with us."

I said, "Well Jim, I'm primarily a B2B specialist. I really don't know anything about retail."

"That's exactly why we want to hire you. A retail consultant is going to tell us what they tell all our competitors. They're going to tell them the same thing. So we're not going to learn anything new or different. You do not come from our world. We want you to come in and teach us what you know, and we'll figure out what's new, and we'll use that."

That gave me that slap-on-the-head reminder of what Edwards Deming had said about benchmarking. And since that time, I've been a strong proponent of this idea. I came up with the term Stealing Genius, in which the idea is to go out and study aliens. And I used the word *alien* because, obviously, it means the people and industry cultures you're studying are foreign to you. It's not unusual to see something that might be common in another industry but doesn't exist in your industry. You have to take that common thing and bring it back into your industry, where it's brand-new. And if you do it right, it's hard to copy.

I've talked about getting into the Uncopyable Mind-Set, which is about trying to use new eyes to see things. You're trying to break away from your own heuristics because we all have our heuristics.

Stealing Genius requires you to put yourself in a position that is uncomfortable and is foreign to you. You study alien organizations and alien experiences.

Besides Delphi, I've taken many of my clients to malls, and at some point we get into the Apple store. I'll say, "When you go in there, don't go in there as the typical consumer you've always been, because when you go as a consumer, you are being manipulated by the experience Apple wants you to have. When you are going to steal genius, you are detaching yourself from that. You are now an alien who is saying, 'I want to study these weird human beings, and I want to study these weird things called businesses.' You go in with a fresh perspective that encourages you to ask yourself what that company is doing to impact your experience, what that company is doing to separate people from their money. You're reappraising the retail experience you're being provided with through that lens—from the first impression to the way the store is laid out to how the products are displayed to the way the staffers are attired. Now you're taking it in differently. You see how the company has made the customer experience unique."

I HAVE FOUR DIFFERENT APPROACHES
TO STEALING GENIUS I TEACH MY CLIENTS.

1. Follow an Objective-Focused Approach

Let's say you run a trade show, and you're not happy with the way customer traffic flows through it. How can you come up with a smarter way to manage traffic, to get more attendees to walk all over the show instead of just stopping at a few booths?

Trade shows are usually a great example of wrong ways to do that. Almost invariably, you've got that inevitable up-and-down aisle layout, and the biggest exhibitors are always right at the front of the hall. Smaller/newer exhibitors are relegated to the fringes where overall traffic is slimmer.

Surely, there's room for improvement. So, if improving traffic flow is the objective here, then who outside our trade-show world is an expert at traffic flow?

Well, supermarkets are really, really good at traffic flow. Think about it for a second. Supermarkets are laid out a lot like a trade-show exhibition space, with the up-and-down aisles. But where do they put milk, the equivalent of their big exhibitor? Practically everyone who comes in is going to grab some milk, just as everyone at a tradeshow is going to be sure to stop by the biggest exhibitor. Do they put the milk at the front of the store, so you can grab it and get out in a hurry?

Nope. *It's at the back of the store. It's a destination.*

It's always the farthest away from the door, forcing you to go through the store to get to it. Supermarkets separate the sections people have to reach and locate them at the four corners of the building. Thus, produce is at one end, meat is at another end, and dairy is at another end. You're being sent around the whole perimeter of the store, forcing you to pass all the other products. The highest-profit-margin products are placed at eye level. The staples, the stuff with lower profit margins, are placed on the bottom row.

Does it work? Well, how many times have you gone to the market just to pick up a quart of milk and come out with a bag full of groceries? Every time?

Las Vegas casinos are a great example of beautifully managed traffic flow. There are no straight lines in a Las Vegas casino. You get lost in them, which is exactly their objective. They force you to walk in a drunken, serpentine fashion around the casino.

These are all prime examples of the objective-focused type of Stealing Genius. If it's traffic flow you want to work on, first we identify the industries we know are really good at this and then study them for best practices.

2. Study Specific Geniuses.

American Girl stores and Disney parks are examples I've used. Companies will go to the Disney Institute to study customer service, but that's not what I'm talking about.

What is Disney really good at? How does Disney attract guests to its parks, for example? How does Disney enhance the experience of a customer? Once you start to study Disney from a perspective like this, you'll begin to see what that company does can be extrapolated to your business.

I've been a huge student of Disney for a long time, and I've had many Stealing Genius laboratories at Disney World. They actually even created a program for me to take my clients to. Among the things we've learned are that when you arrive at Disney World or even Disneyland, the first thing you notice is you can't actually see inside the park from outside the gates. You come up to the gates, and the first thing you see is a beautiful garden area with a giant Mickey Mouse "portrait" made up of flowering plants.

That's designed to be your first photo opportunity. Most people stop and take a picture in front of Mickey, setting the tone for their visit. If you look down, you'll notice the concrete you're walking on is red like a giant red carpet, welcoming you. Then, you have to pass through a dark tunnel to enter the park. The length of this tunnel is lined with big pictures—fake movie posters, really—of the rides you'll see inside. These previews of coming attractions, if you will, build your anticipation for what's ahead. Then—boom—you're out of the tunnel and into the bright sunlight, standing on Main Street, Disney's homage to the nostalgic past of small-town Americana. You stand there, and from that vantage point, you can see Sleeping Beauty's castle. What you're less likely to notice is the artists and designers who created Main Street used the technique called forced perspective to make it all look bigger and, magically, further away, pulling your gaze down the street to the very top of the seemingly distant castle's turret.

As you walk by the bakery shop, your mouth waters at the scent of cookies baking—but there are no ovens in the shop. The cookies are actually baked several miles away and brought there, but Disney has vents installed on the outside of the bakery, out of which the smell of freshly baked cookies is piped into the outside air. The popcorn machines do the same thing.

And have you ever noticed as you're walking through a Disney park that the line of demarcation between the different lands—Fantasyland, Frontier Land—is subtly indicated by a slow change in the texture of the ground under your feet? Or have you ever seen anyone in the wrong costume for the "land" they're in? There's never a Tomorrow Land employee walking through Frontier Land, because that would be incongruent. An elaborate system of tunnels and corridors underneath the Magic Kingdom is where they disappear. This *utilidor*, as Disney calls it, is out of the public's view, allowing cast members to move through the park unseen.

But most people don't notice these details. They just feel the seamless smoothness of the Disney experience, without really understanding the level of effort, art, and mindfulness that go into creating that experience.

And that, of course, is the point.

They're never done innovating, by the way. That's the other thing I've realized in the fifty or so trips I've taken.

I could go on and on, but my point is you're going somewhere. Whether it's the American Girl store, whether it's Disney, whether it's Las Vegas, or it's Wegman's grocery store, it just doesn't matter. Go to companies you can see are well run, and look for ideas to steal.

Having read this far, you won't be surprised to learn my third approach.

3. Ask Yourself, What Would Disney Do?

It doesn't have to literally be Disney. Any highly successful and unique company can stand in for Disney.

I do an exercise with clients in which I ask them to name a great company, and maybe they'll mention Apple.

I'll say, "Great. If Apple were to come in and buy your company, what would Apple do to make your company more successful?" If they say, "Disney," my question is, "What would Disney do to make your company more successful?" or "What would FedEx do if it were to buy your company? What kind of an approach would it take? What would it change? What would Cirque du Soleil do?"

"Well, it would be totally crazy." And they'll come up with some notions of what that kind of *crazy* might look like.

Then I ask them, "Why don't you do that?"

"Because it would go against industry norms."

I say, "Yeah, and the problem is what?"—because, again, people get stuck in their own heuristics. But the moment you start going through an exercise like this, clients start out by saying, "We want to be different. We want to be seen as different from everybody else."

Do they? Do you?

Try it. Just think of somebody. What would Steven Spielberg do? What would Steve Jobs have done if he had taken over your business? What about Mary Kay Ash or Jeff Bezos? Think of people you admire. If they came in and were advising you, what would they suggest?

I use these first three exercises with clients all the time, but the fourth approach, the most important and the most powerful piece of Stealing Genius, *is to develop a habit of active awareness* of Stealing Genius.

4. Develop a Habit of Active Awareness.

What do I mean by that? It means I want your radar up, wherever you are, and always alert for ideas. You're asking and answering these questions: What's different about how their company does business? How are they communicating with customers? How are they directing people? How are they marketing to people? What are they doing with their products that we're not doing with our products? That's the homework I assign clients, and it's intended to create a habit, something they'll do without thinking about it once it's ingrained.

When I come back after a series of training sessions with clients, we'll typically all go out for lunch or dinner somewhere. Once we're all seated and comfortable, I'll say, "Let's go around the table. Everybody at this table, tell me something you've observed at this restaurant about how they do business." It's always interesting; once I've asked them that question, they'll say, "Well, when we walked in, here's how they greeted us," or "I noticed that you don't really see bussers here."

"Okay. Is that something you can steal?" What I'm looking to create is permanent awareness. And, interestingly, a lot of my clients are so in the habit of doing this now that they can't go anywhere without making this kind of mindful observation. But I've also planted something that helps them, and this all works together because, as much as I want people to remember this, people do forget.

That's why I always remind them, "The color orange is a trigger. It's a subconscious trigger that reminds you that you want to be Uncopyable, that you should observe things you may be able to steal, and you should look for things you can observe for ten minutes."

And it works. That's why I call it a trigger. Not only does orange make my clients think of me but it also reminds them to steal genius.

Can you see how all of this fits together?

Orange is not just my brand color; it's tied to the innovation strategy and the experience strategy I teach. None of these are independent of the others; they work together.

You've got to create the triggers and anchors that feed into your branding proposition, your promise. In the next chapter, I'll dig into creating your club, that exclusive velvet-roped space your VIP customers will never want to leave and your less-valuable customers will be begging to get into.

BONUS CONTENT AND
WORKBOOK AVAILABLE AT
UNCOPYABLETHEBOOK.COM

CHAPTER FIVE

Uncopyable Experience

Were you a member of the Mickey Mouse Club? I was. I had the ears. When I had the ears on, watching the program on TV, I felt I really belonged to something. I felt I was one of the cool kids.

In some form or other, most of us want to be one of the cool kids. Growing up, many of us tried to be a part of the cool kids at school. We felt better about ourselves if we were. It's different for adults, but there is still a great attraction. Harley owners are cool kids. Golfers with the newest Callaway driver are cool kids. Wearing the Apple watch or a Fitbit puts you in the cool-kids category. Every one of these is an example of attachment.

There are five critical pieces that go into creating attachment. The first one is that people who are in your inner circle are treated as cool kids and are, automatically, members of the cool-kids club. As long as they're in the club, they get cool stuff and all the perks of cool-kid-dom, but if they leave, they don't get that stuff anymore. So there's a penalty for leaving, and it can be built up into what I consider the most powerful way to deliver an Uncopyable experience and get people attached: creating a club everybody wants to be a member of.

Do you know about Club 33? It's a secret private club inside Disneyland, right next to the Pirates of the Caribbean ride. The only way you'd know it's there is a door with the number thirty-three on it.

But when you go inside, you discover an amazing experience. Not only is Club 33 the best restaurant in Orange County, California, but it's also the only place on Disneyland property that serves alcohol. The food is spectacular, but it's the ambiance that's really amazing. There are framed Walt Disney cartoons all over the place, along with some of his personal effects, such as his piano. It's very, very, very cool. You can go in there in cut-offs, and I've seen people there in tuxedos. I've seen movie stars there, and I've seen royalty there, and everybody's happy to be at Club 33. The last time I checked, the wait for membership was about ten years. When you're taken there, no matter who you are, it's a thrill. If you're a guest, you'll wish you were one of the Club 33 cool kids.

Disney totally rules at this kind of thing. No corporation is more loyal to its fans. Apart from the exclusive Club 33, Disney also has a club for grown-up Disney fanatics called D23, an insider's reference to the start-up date of the Disney studio in 1923. It doesn't cost much to be a member—just $75 a year—but once you pay your nominal dues, you're a member of the club. You get a glossy magazine full of the kind of inside scoops on the parks and the movies Disneyphiles live for. You're offered special events including trips to the Disney lot in California, movie screenings, and exclusive premieres of coming attractions. You get to meet legendary Disney animators and purchase special, exclusive merchandise. Disney has massive conventions that draw thousands of attendees. D23 was the brainchild of the then studio head Robert Iger, who created this "first official community for Disney fans" in 2009 to make them feel they were "part of the magic"—in other words, one of the cool kids.

Where do you think those people go on vacation? And what do you think they tell their friends about the experience?

Maker's Mark bourbon has its Ambassadors' Club. When you join, you get business cards declaring you a Maker's Mark ambassador, and the company sends you cool stuff to share with others. Your name is engraved on a brass plate on a new barrel. After it has aged for two to three years, you can go to Loretto, Kentucky, and get two bottles printed with your name on the label from your barrel. Every Christmas, the company sends you a gift—for instance, a stocking cap for your bottle of Maker's Mark. The Maker's Mark distillery in Kentucky holds special events for members. The CEO told me upward of five thousand people show up, and they're all ambassadors.

That tangible stuff you give your cool kids—your version of the moose whistle or Mont Blanc pen—is delivered to them as an enhancement to the relationship, something to reinforce your branding. When you were a kid and you sent away for the decoder ring or put on your Mickey Mouse Club ears, you were part of something and the ring or the ears or whatever was your physical link to it was the thing that gave you that small thrill of membership and ownership.

The airlines' frequent-prisoner programs are possibly the most successful example of this kind of club. I've flown primarily American Airlines my whole life. The year the frequent-prisoner program started I signed up, so now I can't leave, because the airline owns me. The loss for me would be too great. I've logged over five million miles on American, and because I'm so high up in the airline's echelon, my miles never expire. But if I were to stop flying with American, it would be "Oh, okay, you stopped, so your miles are going to expire next year." And then I'm screwed. I'm not a cool kid anymore.

That's a club, and no industry is more successful at making it look very disadvantageous to leave its clubs than the airline industry.

Cool-kids clubs aren't just for the Disneys, Maker's Marks, and American Airlines. I work with Incisive Computing, a small company that develops software for the portable data-storage industry. When we first started working together, the company wanted to increase demand for its software and also be able to continually improve the product for the marketplace. But how could we create an *Uncopyable Attachment?*

The first thing we did was to rebrand the company's positioning in the marketplace. It specializes in a niche business—a small but rich niche. Its biggest competition comes from larger companies for whom this particular area is just a small segment in their larger business. It made sense, then, to brand Incisive as the specialist in the industry. This is what Incisive does. This is all it does, and it has more experience and expertise in this business than anyone else.

But in branding itself as a specialist, Incisive has to limit the number of customers it can take on in order to maintain a high-quality product and high-quality customer service. (Can you see where this is going?)

So, the company's message is that in order for it to deliver the highest level of product and service, it must limit its customer base to a set number of companies. If you want to become one of its customers, it will put you on the waiting list, and when a client leaves, the next company in line can come in. Scarcity plus exclusivity equals its version of the cool-kids club.

Then I said, "Look, your prices have to be the premium price because you're the specialist, and you can only work with so many companies." At the annual trade show, this company has a meeting just for its users, who are presented with logo merchandise to remind them of the benefits of being in this elite-users group.

And if people decide to leave the club, then have regrets and want to come back? Tough.

Get at the back of the line. They're kicking butt with this strategy. Following the Uncopyable, actionable marketing steps and ideas resulted in doubling their trade-show leads and a 56 percent year-to-date increase in subscription revenue.

To me, the club is one of the coolest things you can create. The club creates that personal, emotional attachment in which the fear of loss is actually greater than almost everything else, along with the perception of especially high value.

I'll bet you belong to a club or two, even if you don't see them that way—and your experience of that product or service is colored by your membership. If you're a Mac person, you're in the club. That's what it is. And for years, it's always been the Mac people against the PC people, and Mac people have always considered themselves to be much cooler. Sure, PCs are the vast majority of

BE THE CLUB ALL YOUR CUSTOMERS AND PROSPECTS WANT TO BE A MEMBER OF.

the marketplace, but the cool kids are over here with Apple. And you would never stop using Macs or iPhones or that stuff because you wouldn't be in the club anymore, and you'd have to find a whole new set of friends.

I like the formalized clubs. I have a club of about eighteen major trade associations I started twenty years ago. We meet three times a year, and I work with them on creating amazing, Uncopyable experiences at their meetings or their trade shows to increase the value of what they're marketing, selling, and sharing. It's a great example of what I teach clients: if you're able to establish a club with your customers, especially your big or influential customers, you can leverage that. In this case, though these associations paid to be members of my club, they hired me as a consultant, I've spoken at all their conferences, I do webinars for these guys, and I'm exposed to their members, their sponsors, and exhibitors. It's been a tremendous help in growing my business.

The second critical piece of creating attachment is to give clients something nobody else has.

There are all kinds of things you can do for your members above and beyond your version of the moose whistle. One great for-members-only perk is *proprietary information or original content that is only shared with customers.* Companies will do surveys or research projects. Then, when they get the data collected, they share it with their customers and nobody else, making certain those valued customers know the data is exclusively for them. Alternatively, a company will sell the research at a very high price but will give it to their customers for free, telling them, "It's our gift to you, one of the exclusive benefits for being our customer."

White papers, videos, and audio podcasts are other kinds of proprietary original content you can share with customers, as are interviews with them you might post on your website or share on YouTube. Some companies offer limited access to these kinds of materials, while making it clear the bulk of them are reserved exclusively for their customers.

If your club is large, consider segmenting it with levels that reward your best customers the most, and give those who spend less something to work toward. The airlines do that: their frequent-prisoner programs—the hotel programs and the rest—are all leveled according to how much and how often a customer spends. (More on this in the next chapter.)

Remember the key to making the club attractive is finding ways to give your customers tangible and intangible rewards that serve the double purpose of making them feel like cool kids and triggering your company's name in their minds whenever they see these rewards.

The third critical piece of creating attachment is to become the Kevin Bacon of your customers' universe.

When you create a club *and you become the facilitator of that group*, then your value is extraordinary. But I also conscientiously cultivated my network in the exhibitions industry because I intended to become the Kevin Bacon of the meetings-and-conventions world.

Remember the party game Six Degrees of Kevin Bacon? Basically, the idea was everyone in Hollywood was only separated from Kevin Bacon by six acquaintances at maximum. The winner of the game is the one who can find the shortest path from any Hollywood figure to Kevin Bacon. For example, Henry Winkler was in the 1998 box-office smash *Ground Control* with an actor named John Neilsen (who?), who was also in the runaway hit *Rails and Ties* with Kevin Bacon in 2007. Winkler has a Bacon number of two. (There are actually websites you can search on Google and play the game!)

For years I was the most closely connected person to anybody in the trade-show industry. People would ask me, "Hey Steve, do you know so-and-so?" And the answer, most of the time, was yes. Usually, it was one degree of separation, sometimes two. That made me extremely valuable to people looking to make contacts, but *only the people in my club had access to that part of what I could do.*

Being a resource, being a connection is also a powerful way to create an experience that's very difficult to copy, if not Uncopyable.

Again, it comes down to defining/creating your own box in the customer's mind, or the prospect's mind, or your industry's mind.

You're creating an experience with people, and you are putting things in your box that reinforce that experience, that enhance it, that are hard to get, *that are in no other box*. It's like saying, "I'm going to create my own rules of competition," as Incisive Computing did by declaring itself to be a specialist that has and maintains a strictly limited client roster. That's its box.

People who want to be in that box will bend over backward. At the same time, it also helps if people say they don't want to be in that box. And Incisive says, just as Harley-Davidson does, "That's fine."

Differentiating and defining yourself can be a challenge if your competition has cornered a specific demographic. In designing its competing theme park, Universal Studios took up the challenge and created a user experience that is very consciously *not* Walt Disney World's. Walt Disney World is "family." That's what it's about. Universal Studios is for teenagers and young adults, with an edgier vibe to the rides and the park design and having restaurants that serve alcohol. They've each created their own boxes—and their own clubs.

The fourth critical piece of creating attachment is to look for the opportunity to do something outside the *product*.

What's the difference between American Airlines, Delta Airlines, and United Airlines?

The answer is . . . *nothing*. There is nothing different. The only thing that attaches you to one of them is membership in their frequent-prisoner program.

But then there's Southwest Airlines, and Southwest Airlines has created an experience. (Gee, I seem to be using them a lot. I wonder why?)

Southwest isn't so much about being a club as it is about being great at creating unique, fun, little "wow" experiences—things that only happen when you're flying with Southwest.

On one occasion, my friend Larry and I were flying from Albuquerque to Phoenix.

When you get on a Southwest plane, the first thing you notice is the flight attendants act as if they want to be there, which is different in and of itself. One flight attendant said to us, "Good morning, guys. Hey, glad to see you. Thanks for coming."

My buddy Larry said to her, "You know, he's a world-famous author."

World-famous author? What the heck are you talking about? I thought.

But she looked at me and asked, "Are you really an author?"

And I said, "Well, yeah."

She said, "Do you have one of your books with you?"

"Yeah."

She said, "Would you give it away as a prize?"

And I said, "Sure. Why not?"

So we take off. Mind you, this is a very short flight, only about forty-five minutes or so. After the flight attendants did their little safety spiel, she took the microphone and said, "Ladies and gentlemen, we are so excited to tell you we have the world-famous author Steve Miller on board our flight today. And he has generously offered an autographed copy of one of his books to the winner of our contest. Here's what the contest is: Take out a piece of paper, write down your seat number, and then write down how many squares of toilet paper you think it will take to go down the aisle from row 1 to row 30. We're going to roll one of the toilet paper rolls down the aisle, and we're going to count how many squares there are. The person who comes the closest will win his book."

Now everyone's laughing, and you can see people trying to figure it out: how big a square was and how long a swath it would take to get down the aisle. They were all writing like crazy, doing the math. As we start to approach Phoenix, the attendant said, "Okay, we need everybody to turn in their answers." Then the flight crew brought out a toilet paper roll, which they rolled down the middle of the aisle, and they counted the number of squares it took. Before we landed in Phoenix, a twelve-year-old kid got an autographed copy of *How to Get the Most Out of Trade Shows*.

You know that kid was just thrilled.

But again, that's a great example of looking for the opportunity to do something that's outside the product. It's all well and good to make it a pleasant ride and smile and pass out pretzels, but the crew entertained us, they engaged us. And you know everybody on that plane told people the story. In fact, I've told that story to audiences many times.

That doesn't happen by accident. That's smart hiring, that's smart training, and that's having the vision to build a corporate culture around creating memorable and very specifically Southwest-style experiences. It didn't cost the airline anything. All it took was one staff member paying attention and grabbing an opportunity to turn a mundane flight into something fun and goofy—and that one person who was paying attention made *me* feel like a rock star.

Which leads us to the fifth critical piece of creating attachment: making your customers into rock stars.

How are you creating rock-star opportunities for your customers?

If you should happen to attend a performance at the gorgeous Sydney Opera House, you would experience one of the most brilliant rock-star-creating strategies I've ever seen—that is, as long as you're driving a Lexus.

You see, they have a valet who handles Lexus cars exclusively. You pull up to the valet, who takes your Lexus and parks it. By itself, it's pretty cool, but there's also a special VIP reception area reserved just for you, the Lexus owner. Welcome!

Driving a Mercedes? Tough. Go park yourself, loser! There is no exclusive velvet-roped reception area for you.

Think about that for a second. If you're someone who goes to the Sydney Opera, and you're a Lexus owner, would you ever consider switching to Mercedes? Probably not, since you're used to getting the rock-star treatment as a Lexus owner. Added attraction? Getting to thumb your nose at the Mercedes people. You're one of the cool kids! For you, driving a Mercedes would be a step down.

Lexus has created an experience above and beyond the product itself. Genius! I talked earlier about the three traditional components of competition that companies based their sales on: product, service, and price. Adding an experience to the relationship your customers have with you kind of wraps around those three, and it magnifies the relationship.

We went through the branding strategy in chapter three and the innovation strategy in chapter four. The branding strategy boils down to what your promise is to people in the marketplace. The innovation strategy is about promising delivery of something valuable and different. What happens as a result of creating this kind of experience is *attachment.*

It's possible you could create a promise for your customer and reinforce it with your anchors and triggers. You could be innovative and fresh, yet still fall short of creating a genuinely personal attachment because creating the experience that leads to personal attachment is the secret sauce of the Uncopyable approach. All those other elements are merely the supporting cast for the star of the show, which is the experience strategy.

I was on a business trip and staying at the Muse Hotel in Manhattan, a small boutique hotel about a block away from Times Square. I was getting ready to leave in the morning to go to a meeting. I was in my bathroom, and I had one of those little travel tubes of toothpaste. It was almost empty, so I squeezed it to get the last dollop out. I brushed my teeth, threw out the empty tube, and made a mental note to be sure to pick up some toothpaste before I came back that night.

I was out all day at meetings, and then, of course, we all went out to dinner, and it got late. It was about 10:30 p.m. when I arrived at the hotel. I got on the elevator, went up to my floor, and as I put my hand on the knob of the door to my room, I realized I had forgotten to get the toothpaste.

Aargh! 10:30 p.m. at night, and I've got to go out and find some toothpaste. Damn.

I went inside to drop my briefcase off and had started to head out again when I happened to glance in the bathroom. Lying on the counter of the bathroom was a new tube of toothpaste and a note from the housekeeper that read, "Dear Mr. Miller, I saw you were out of toothpaste. I didn't want you to have to worry about it, so I took the liberty of replacing it for you. Hope you're enjoying your stay. —Marsha"

Wow! I'm in the business of wow, and yet I was wowed.

Go to the Muse Hotel's website and you'll see its branding promise: "We love harnessing the energy of the city in our hotel, but we also have a relaxed, reflective side. Our thinking caps are always on as we imagine ways to keep things fresh and welcoming for you."

If I had read that before I'd stayed there, I'd probably have shrugged it off. How many times have you been told how much you were valued and promised—"We're going to go above and beyond . . ."—and all that stuff? And how many times has that been a crock?

But they were saying, "We always keep our thinking caps on," and finding that toothpaste was a wow experience for me that showed they meant it.

A little tube of toothpaste.

I've told that story hundreds of times in front of tens of thousands of people around the world. I've asked people, "Has this ever happened to you?" and nobody has said yes. People simply cannot believe it—"Wow, that's an amazing experience." Yet what we're talking about is just a little tube of toothpaste that cost about a buck.

Clearly, the people who run the Muse made this promise and had asked themselves, "Okay, how do we deliver on this?" The delivery was in training their staff to be on the lookout for the opportunity to be amazing, for the opportunity to create a wow experience.

I was speaking at the Ritz Carlton in Naples, Florida, and thought I'd test a five-star hotel. I deliberately squeezed out all the toothpaste from my tube and threw it away because I wanted to see what would happen—and I was speaking there the next morning.

Nothing happened.

So I got up in front of my audience and said, "Here we are, staying in this five-star resort . . ." Yes, the place was incredible, and I can't deny it had great customer service. But here was an opportunity for the Ritz Carlton to do something amazing. And the hotel staff didn't do it. For me, that made my experience at the Muse that much more special.

Here's the thing: *A richly imprinted experience wants to be repeated. It wants to be remembered. And it wants to be shared.*

The more impressive your great experience is for people, the better it's going to be for you. And all it might take is a travel tube of toothpaste, ninety-six cents on Amazon.

There are a few good ways to approach this: One is to put your radar up (as in Stealing Genius, covered in chapter four) and study how other successful companies have created a memorable customer experience.

When I'm speaking, I'll often ask my audience, "What's the world's most ridden roller coaster?" I get all kinds of answers but almost never the correct one, which is Space Mountain in Walt Disney World.

Space Mountain is just a roller coaster, but it's wrapped in a unique and compelling experience. Disney has done that with Splash Mountain and Big Thunder Railroad too. All are just roller coasters, but all are wrapped in an experience and an added layer of storytelling and effects that make them into something greater and more engaging than your ordinary thrill ride. Disney has created an experience that begins when you're standing in line, as does the experience at all the big attractions at Disney parks. Music and stagecraft are building your anticipation and immersing you into the world Disney is creating for you before you step foot on a ride.

Creating an unexpected moment of wow is one way to approach creating the experience. It's not easy to do, because you have to educate yourself and your frontline staff to be constantly aware of what the customer is experiencing and then look for the opportunity to do something great.

A little bit ago, I was in Charleston, South Carolina, staying at the downtown Courtyard Marriott. I happened to walk by the front desk where I saw a couple talking to the manager. The woman was sobbing and wiping her eyes as she spoke. Her husband had his arm around her, but I noticed he was smiling. I overheard the woman saying, "That was so nice, thank you so much. We can't tell you how much we appreciate it." Whatever it was, it had clearly moved her tremendously.

When they finally walked away from the desk, I approached the manager and said, "Pardon me for butting in, but I couldn't help but overhear." I'd been there a few times, so he knew who I was and what I did. "I heard her thanking you over and over. Do you mind if I ask you what you did?"

He shrugged, "Oh, it's no big deal."

"Clearly, it was a big deal to her. What did you do?"

"Well, it's their anniversary, and I thought I'd just do something nice. I sent a bottle of champagne to their room, a couple glasses, and a little card that said, 'We certainly appreciate you spending your anniversary with us, and we hope you'll enjoy this bottle of champagne on us.'"

That was all he did. But whenever this couple comes to Charleston again, you can bet they're going to be staying at the Courtyard every single time. And they're going to tell everybody they know about that experience and how great the Courtyard is all because the manager saw an opportunity to give them a great experience and stepped up.

This is why people have to be trained to look for the opportunities to create world-class wow moments in which they make their customers feel like rock stars, as I mentioned earlier. In the next chapter, I'll talk about how you can create rock stars of your own and why you should want to.

BONUS CONTENT AND
WORKBOOK AVAILABLE AT
UNCOPYABLETHEBOOK.COM

SECTION

THREE
THREE
THREE
THREE
THREE

UNCOPYABLE TOOLS AND RULES

CHAPTER SIX

Creating Rock Stars

There's a reason why we come up with ways to celebrate our club members out loud, and it's to incentivize them to strive to become one of the very special few, the ones I call my rock stars. My rock stars are the standouts among my BFFs. They're unswerving in their referrals, their endorsements, and their loyalty. They are worth their weight in gold.

What would it take to make someone want to be one of *your* brand's rocks stars?

To explain this, let's look at Abraham Maslow's famous hierarchy of needs. Maslow survived incarceration as a prisoner of war in a German concentration camp in World War II. When he got out, he was consumed by the question of why some people survived the camps and others did not. To explain it, he came up with this construct he called the hierarchy of needs.

Essentially, it's a pyramid with five different levels, the bottom and largest one being the most rudimentary needs: your basic food and care. The second level is safety and feeling safe in your environment. The third level is love and belonging (as in the club concept I talked about). We all fall into that instinctively. Golfers hang with golfers. People who knit hang out with people who knit. Like attracts like.

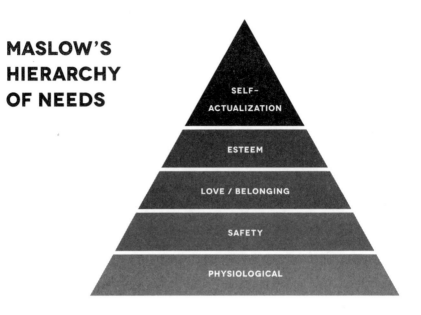

MASLOW'S HIERARCHY OF NEEDS

SELF-ACTUALIZATION

ESTEEM

LOVE / BELONGING

SAFETY

PHYSIOLOGICAL

The fourth level is self-esteem, feeding the ego. Two of the biggest things that reinforce a person's self-esteem are, number one, to be *appreciated* for who you are and what you do, and number two, to be *recognized* for who you are and what you do.

In short, your customers want to feel like rock stars. They want to be *on* the stage, not working behind it or sitting in the audience.

They want to be Beyoncé. They want to be The Boss. They want to be appreciated and recognized—by you.

How do you make your customers feel like rock stars?

Through VIP treatment, of course. And the more important people are to you and your business, the more special their treatment should be.

Look at the awards that matter in show business: the Academy Awards, the Emmys, the Grammys, the Tonys. These are the celebrations of excellence by and within affinity groups: actors/actresses, performers, singers, dancers, musicians. Now, to us, these people are already at the top of their profession. Why in the world would a dumb statuette mean anything to someone with, say, Meryl Streep's track record?

The reason these awards matter is they are awarded by peers. Public recognition, coupled with peer respect and a physical manifestation of that respect that can be taken home—such as an Oscar—is a big deal, even for a world-famous movie star.

When my daughter, Kelly, was very small, we took her to Disney World for her birthday, and we paid for one of those Disney birthday parties. It wasn't a big roomful of kids—just us and a couple of the costumed princess characters who came in and made a fuss over her. Of course, they were just pretty college girls playing parts, but for Kelly, this was the real deal; Cinderella was celebrating *her.* That made her feel very, very special, I promise you.

And not only was a real, live princess wishing her a happy birthday, but Kelly also got to wear a special crown at the Magic Kingdom that day. People would see her and say, "Where'd you get that crown?"

And she'd say, "It's my birthday. Cinderella gave it to me."

She was a rock star.

If you can make your customers feel like a six-year-old birthday girl in a princess crown hanging out at Disney World with Cinderella, believe me, they won't forget it.

ACKNOWLEDGE. RECOGNIZE. REWARD. REPEAT.

Rock stars love the spotlight. Don't be stingy with it.

Whenever I hold meetings with clients, I make sure to acknowledge and recognize my rock stars for the things they did for me. If, for instance, one of them referred me to a new client or talked up my business in a magazine interview, that person might find a nice shiny limo waiting to pick them up at the airport and whisk them to the hotel where the meeting is being held. It has a nice, out-loud gesture of appreciation and the extra bonus of having that person show up and innocently ask everyone else, "Oh, did you get a limo? Did everybody get a limo?" The answer is no, not everybody got a limo, but a few of you did because you're my rock stars.

Here's another example: I once got a call from Tom Conley, who was then the CEO for what's now the International Housewares Association. He said, "I have a major trade show our association owns and runs. It's one of the top ten trade shows in the United States. We have two thousand exhibiting companies, we have two hundred on the waiting list, and we have sixteen thousand attendees. It appears to be very healthy, but I'm nervous as hell and I don't know why. Can I hire you to come in and do an analysis of the show and kind of see if I'm out of my mind or something?"

I came in and did the analysis. As it turned out, we did find cracks in the armor, nearly invisible cracks that if left unrepaired could have killed the whole trade show. We made some important changes. A few months after word got around about what we'd done, the *Association Management Magazine*, which was the top trade magazine in the association world, contacted me and asked to interview me about it.

I thought about it and I said no. I suggested, instead, that the magazine interview Tom Conley, but I added I'd be happy to write a sidebar for the piece. The magazine editors loved the idea, and the story and Tom's interview wound up on the cover. This was great for Tom. Here he was, getting this tremendous recognition in the association world and, of course, in his interview, he talked about me.

But *he* was the rock star. And that was my point.

Never, ever miss an opportunity to turn the spotlight on your rock stars.

I do weekly short videos that I put out to my BFFs. (They're not my followers, they're not my friends, they're not my family, they're my BFFs.) If people share one of my posts on LinkedIn or something, I acknowledge them in a video: "Hey, a big shout out to Jenny because she shared an article I wrote. Just wanted to tell you how much I appreciate you and thanks a lot for doing that." I'm making her a rock star.

This enhances the experience that people have with you. It's not just some dumb gift basket and a thank-you note. It's public recognition and sincere appreciation for what they're doing. It makes them shine.

Sometimes, you make those opportunities and sometimes it's serendipity. You just need to be ready to grab on to them. I couldn't have predicted or created the opportunity for my client to be on a magazine cover in a story touting my contribution. You can, sometimes, create those moments, so be open and ready to creatively acknowledge your rock stars. But you also need to keep your radar up for unexpected opportunities like that.

I have a good friend who speaks about customer service, Shep Hyken, the author of the best-selling book *Amaze Every Customer Every Time*. Shep also happens to be a world-class magician. My daughter has known him since she was a kid and calls him Mr. Magic. When he comes to town, we always try to get together for dinner, and Kelly always wants him to do a magic show. One time, as we were finishing our dinner, he actually got up in the middle of a restaurant and started doing a magic show. By the time he was halfway through his little show, the entire restaurant was watching him and really enjoying it. He was including Kelly in his act, and she loved it.

Later on, when I was planning a series of marketing webinars for a client, I said, "I'd like to do an interview with this buddy of mine who is a top-drawer, customer-service expert. I think it would be a really great opportunity for your customers to learn more about this." They were very enthusiastic, so I brought Shep on and did an interview with him. He shared outstanding content with the audience, and I was able to promote his speaking and his books during the interview. Since I was doing the promoting, not him, it didn't come off as a hard-sell pitch. It was my chance to give him the rock-star treatment, and I made sure to keep him center stage. (Of course, he's doing the same thing for me for this book!)

Once you glom on to the idea opportunities like this are out there, you'll see them pop up everywhere. *Use them.* Create the attachment, the golden handcuffs. Make them want to work with you because they appreciate you for how you make them feel, like my little girl at Disney World in a princess crown, having a birthday party with her BFF Cinderella.

Your rock stars can be a part of your club, but the treatment they get has to go above and beyond what would normally be expected as a benefit of membership. You've got to elevate them among their peers and show your appreciation and recognition.

Want more illustrations? The Food Network is a perfect example of creating rock stars; I mean, who had ever heard of Rachael Ray before the Food Network created Rachael Ray as a rock star?

Bass Pro Shops create their own rock stars, expert fishermen and women who are featured on Bass Pro's website and brought out to their special events to do demonstrations.

Fiskars, the company that makes those orange-handled scissors, has a club called the Fiskateers. (Where in the heck did the company get the idea for that name?) Fiskars started it up because it realized a lot of women used their scissors for crafts and sewing—and they were using them in groups, little communities of crafters who got together to make things on a regular basis. So, if you join the Fiskateers, you get your own special pair of scissors. Instead of having a typical orange handle, one loop is green and the other is orange. They set users apart when crafting with their friends. When a club member shows up and pulls out those scissors, everybody says, "Oh, you're a Fiskateer."

The company offers these special club members the chance of being on the official advisory board, a small group of people who are the ambassadors for Fiskars's scissors and Fiskars's products for a year. These women are featured on the Fiskateer's website. The women who are the ambassadors are sent around the country as representatives. Mind you, they're normal people, not well-known chefs or hunters. They just happen to love crafts, and they got chosen for that year—and so they're rock stars.

That's it—that's all it takes.

Several of my trade-association clients have created rock stars at trade shows and industry events. Several years ago, we started to pick out people in the manufacturing industry, people who might have small machine shops in small-town, rural America. We'd get comments from them about how they'd attended the International Manufacturing Technology Show, what they got from it, and how it helped their shops. Then we blasted those comments out on the Internet and in magazines and in advertising so when these people came to the trade show, giant signs, signage, and graphics with their pictures blown up on them would be all over the place. For example, a graphic would picture "Bob and Bill from Columbus, Indiana," and now these guys are walking around the trade show. People recognize them and want to get their picture taken with them. To you and me, they're normal, ordinary machinists, but in the manufacturing world, they're rock stars.

And you know what else?

These guys will attend the International Manufacturing Technology Show for the rest of their lives.

HGTV is making rock stars out of people who were just local remodelers or construction workers or designers. When people at HGTV hear about a professional in the field—that she has a winning personality, or he's especially creative at what he does—they go out and do a show about that person and showcase that person's work. All of a sudden, those previously unknown people have a fan base of viewers who want to see more of them. They're rock stars.

Obviously, the music industry has its rock stars, as does the movie industry and professional sports. But that doesn't mean you can't have rock stars in your world, no matter how big it is. In fact, I used to do a speech titled "How to Be a Big Fish in a Small but Rich Pond," which was intended to help people make themselves into rock stars. But the better thing, in my opinion, is to be the person who *creates* rock stars. If I can help people to be more successful, if I can help them to be more recognized, to be better appreciated—well, they will know how that happened, and they'll remember who did it for them.

What do you make when you create rock stars? You create people who, basically, have your anchor or trigger installed in them.

Couple that with the tangible anchors and triggers I talked about in previous chapters because that's what makes this strategy—the creation of Uncopyable Attachment—so powerful. The more of these pieces you're able to incorporate into your business, the more powerful the connections and the more powerful the attachment your customers have with you. You've created your own BFF, fan for life, and ambassador.

The key is making people feel valuable and valued. You're not asking them to recognize your excellence; *you're recognizing theirs* and helping them onto the stage and into the spotlight.

Nobody forgets that feeling.

They'll never leave. They'll just never leave.

BONUS CONTENT AND
WORKBOOK AVAILABLE AT
UNCOPYABLETHEBOOK.COM

CHAPTER SEVEN

Breakthrough Referrals

What do you get in return from your BFFs when you create a cool-kids club for them? Most importantly, you get *referrals*.

When I was in college, at the University of Arizona in Tucson, part of what I did to pay my bills was work as a DJ at a small, local, radio station, KIKX Radio, AM radio. It was just a Top 40, rock 'n roll station—not very big.

One day, the station manager called all the DJs in for a meeting. "You guys are going to sell advertising during your time slot." He made it clear if we didn't do it, we probably wouldn't be DJs there much longer.

None of us were in a position to say no—there were no rock stars in our ranks—but most of us had no sales experience at all, myself included. I thought, *Geez, how do I go about becoming a salesperson?*

I went to a bookstore and bought several books on how to sell. One of the key elements to successful selling, according to these books, was sheer, dogged persistence; the more persistent you were, the more successful you would be. While I didn't cherish the idea of cold calling, I did want to keep getting paychecks. So I started knocking on doors.

I'd make my pitch, and people would say no, and I'd come back a week later and they'd *still* say no. It just went on and on and on. But there was one poor guy who owned a pet store. I wore him down with my endless sales calls, to the point where he caved and said, "Okay, all right. I'll buy some ads. I'll buy some ads."

Luckily for him, we were a small station and our ad rates were cheap. A thirty-second ad during my time slot was about $10, so for $200, he pretty much owned one of my time slots. As I said, I'd beaten the guy down past the point of resistance, so we signed the contract.

Another thing I read in all of these sales books was about the power of referrals and how getting referrals would really help build my sales. The books all offered the same advice about how to get referrals too: "The best time to ask for a referral is right after you make the first sale." So even as this poor guy was signing the ad contract, I gave him a big smile and asked, "So, do you have any friends you would recommend me to?"

He sat back in his chair, looked at me, and laughed out loud. "But, Steve, they're my friends!" As soon as he said that to me, I thought, *Man, this is just not the right way to do this.* There had to be a better way.

As the years went on and I got more into sales and marketing, I would still read these books and articles on selling. Even recently, I was reading a piece online in which a top sales trainer who has books out on this topic (and who shall go nameless) said, "Here is my exact referral plan."

He laid out six steps to getting more referrals. Here they are verbatim:

1. Make a list of the names of your ten best customers.

2. Contact each person on your list and ask to be recommended to their friends, family, and so on.

3. Offer an incentive to those customers who send you a referral.

4. Ask other business owners and professionals to recommend you to their customers.

5. Offer special discounts or other incentives to businesses that send you referrals.

6. Use holidays as a time to offer special incentives for giving you referrals.

Sounds like a lot of other referral program steps I've read over the years. Am I going to follow these steps? There isn't a chance in hell I'm going to do that!

Why not, you ask?

I did a survey of my BFFs a couple of years ago, in which I asked my BFFs what percentage of their business came from referrals. I got a few thousand responses to this question and found an average of 45.15 percent of the survey participants' business came from referrals. Wow! Almost half!

But the follow-up question I asked was, "Do you have a formal referral strategy?" And 73.2 percent of the survey participants said no. So I asked, "Okay, why don't you have a referral strategy?" And the number-one answer was "Because asking for referrals is very uncomfortable."

Why won't I follow those six steps listed previously?

Because it makes me uncomfortable to ask, and it makes my client uncomfortable to hear.

My BFFs said 45 percent of their annual business came from referrals. About 80 percent of my business comes from referrals, so clearly, referrals are critical to the health of my enterprise. For anything that represents such a huge a portion of your business, you ought to have a system in place. But what is the best way to do that?

As I considered the answer, I was actually going down two different paths of thought. I wondered how to create an Uncopyable Attachment with my clients and how to create a referral-marketing system that didn't scare the crap out of me or the people I was trying to get referrals from.

One day, a few years ago, the answer hit me: It was the same strategy! I could use the Uncopyable strategy to actually create a referral strategy! As soon as that epiphany struck, it became very clear.

Let me lay it out for you.

The purpose of business is to create and maintain long-term customer relationships. So we create a relationship with a customer whom we want to stay with us.

Right?

I also believe the purpose of marketing is for your company, product, or service to be on the mind of the prospect when the prospect is ready to buy. The hardest sale you can make is to prospects you believe need your product when *they* don't think they need your product. We have all experienced having to deal with some annoying person who keeps trying to sell us something when we have no desire for, or interest in, what they're selling.

It doesn't matter what that person says to you. *You're never going to buy.*

That's the hardest sale to make. The easiest sale is when the prospects agree they have a need for your product or service.

If you identify people who fit the profile of your target market and you stay in contact with them on a regular basis, using some of the tools we talked about, then when a lightning bolt comes out of the sky and strikes them in the middle of the head, they'll say, "Wow,

I need this . . . oh, who should I . . . oh, Steve Miller!" Right? *Because you're on the mind of the prospect when the prospect is ready to buy.*

So how does this connect to referral marketing, you ask? One distinction to understand is referral marketing is not the same as word-of-mouth marketing. Word-of-mouth marketing is a proactive endorsement *without* an acknowledged need. An example might be that I go to a restaurant for the first time, and this restaurant just blows me away. I get on Facebook the next day and tell everyone, "We went to this restaurant. It was amazing. Everybody who reads this has to go to this restaurant!" In this case, I'm giving a proactive endorsement to everybody, whether they might be interested or not. This is word of mouth; I'm just shouting it out there to whoever's listening.

Referral marketing is a proactive endorsement when there is an acknowledged need, the idea being if the purpose of marketing is to be on the mind of the prospect when the prospect is ready to buy, the purpose of referral marketing is to be on the mind of a current *customer* when somebody they know is ready to buy.

For example, you say to me, "I would like to take my family out to a nice restaurant this weekend, but I'd really like to find somewhere new." I say to you, "Oh, Kay and I went to this restaurant and it was amazing." You've acknowledged you want to find a new restaurant, and I'm now recommending this amazing restaurant. That's a referral. A referral is marketing through a customer.

For this to work, you've got to have three things going for you. First, *your customers have to want to refer you.* You've delivered something especially great and memorable, and you've got their loyalty.

The second thing is *they have to remember you at that moment.* As in the example, when you and I are talking and you say, "I'd love to find a great new restaurant," if I didn't remember that restaurant

I'd visited, then I would just be nodding my head. You need to use the tools I've discussed throughout the book to help your customers remember you, to keep your product or service on their mind.

The third part of it is you must also provide *them* with their own tools, which they can then give to prospects. When people have had a great experience with a company or an individual, they're always happy to make a referral. First, they're happy to promote that person or company as thanks for a job well done. Second, a referral is a subtle way of bragging, of saying, "Hey, look, I found this really great guy who does talks about how to make yourself unique in the marketplace, and you should think about getting in touch with him. He really helped us out." Not only are they helping their friend but they also get to sneak in a little pat on their own back for discovering this great solution. We just have to make it as easy for them as possible.

How? By giving them tools. Here are the five *Uncopyable referral tools* I've found most effective.

1. Help Your Customer's Customer Be Successful.

If you help your customers' customer be successful, your customer will be thrilled. For instance, I'll often ask clients, "Do you ever do webinars for your customers?" More often than not they'll say yes. I'll ask, "And are they about your products?" And their answer is "Yeah, it's all about us."

But it doesn't have to be all about you. Have you ever thought about doing a webinar that helps your customers—a sales webinar, for instance, or a marketing webinar, or a time-management webinar? Maybe your customers' customers have issues with time management. If you could help them help their customers, they'd be grateful, right? You could say to your customers, "I've set up an interview with somebody who's a time-management specialist, and I'd like to give that to *your* customers."

Does your customer already do webinars? If you're an expert in an area of interest to their customers, you can be interviewed on their webinar. That helps them and you. Having you on their webinar is, in effect, an endorsed referral: "I brought him on to talk to you, so clearly I think he knows what he's talking about, and I've hired him myself."

Most of my clients do webinars or videos, usually produced in-house and usually pretty dry. So I'll suggest, "Look, how about I interview you about your business, and you can use the video as an introduction to your new prospects?" Since I'm a professional and I know what I'm doing, we can prep in advance and get our questions together. I can introduce the client, and we can talk. During the course of the conversation, we have a very brief back and forth about how we work together and how I'm a marketing consultant. And— voila!—another endorsed referral.

2. Provide Your Customers with Articles or Newsletters.

You can provide useful, informative, and unique content your customers can share with their customers. E-mail newsletters can be good, but I prefer actual, physical newsletters. Next to face-to-face, direct mail is probably the most powerful marketing tool you can use. Send them extra copies and suggest they hand them out to people they know or with whom they do business.

One of my clients started a newsletter two years ago and recently told me he had no idea a newsletter could be so powerful.

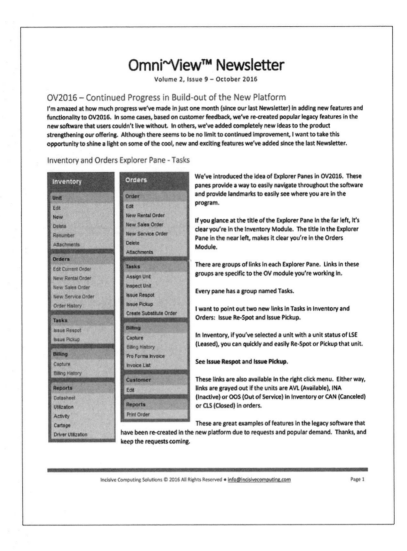

Omni~View™ Newsletter
Volume 2, Issue 9 – October 2016

OV2016 – Continued Progress in Build-out of the New Platform
I'm amazed at how much progress we've made in just one month (since our last Newsletter) in adding new features and functionality to OV2016. In some cases, based on customer feedback, we've re-created popular legacy features in the new software that users couldn't live without. In others, we've added completely new ideas to the product strengthening our offering. Although there seems to be no limit to continued improvement, I want to take this opportunity to shine a light on some of the cool, new and exciting features we've added since the last Newsletter.

Inventory and Orders Explorer Pane - Tasks

We've introduced the idea of Explorer Panes in OV2016. These panes provide a way to easily navigate throughout the software and provide landmarks to easily see where you are in the program.

If you glance at the title of the Explorer Pane in the far left, it's clear you're in the Inventory Module. The title in the Explorer Pane in the near left, makes it clear you're in the Orders Module.

There are groups of links in each Explorer Pane. Links in these groups are specific to the OV module you're working in.

Every pane has a group named Tasks.

I want to point out two new links in Tasks in Inventory and Orders: Issue Re-Spot and Issue Pickup.

In Inventory, if you've selected a unit with a unit status of LSE (Leased), you can quickly and easily Re-Spot or Pickup that unit.

See Issue Respot and Issue Pickup.

These links are also available in the right click menu. Either way, links are grayed out if the units are AVL (Available), INA (Inactive) or OOS (Out of Service) in Inventory or CAN (Canceled) or CLS (Closed) in orders.

These are great examples of features in the legacy software that have been re-created in the new platform due to requests and popular demand. Thanks, and keep the requests coming.

3. Live Events Create Great Referral Opportunities.

This could be a live event you put on yourself—a customer appreciation day, a demo day, or an open house day—or part of a larger event. In either case, you have to make your event Uncopyable by making it memorable and unusual.

For example, a company I was working with had me speak for them at a special invitational meeting for their top twenty-five customers. For two days, I spoke on marketing for an hour each morning and gave them lots of great information, which effectively legitimized the learning experience for these people. But it's what they did *afterward* that made the experience Uncopyable.

After I spoke on the first morning, this company took their special guests golfing. It was nice, and everyone enjoyed it, but it was not unique. On the second day, however, they took everybody to do the Richard Petty Driving Experience at one of the NASCAR raceways. Everybody got to put on their fire suits and drive these six hundred horsepower NASCAR racing machines. Not only did they get to have an adrenaline-pumping, unforgettable experience, but they also had their pictures taken with their cars, and those pictures were passed out as mementoes. You *know* people are going to go home and talk about that. And their colleagues and friends are going to ask, "Wow, why did they take you there?"

"Oh, I'm a customer of theirs. They take really good care of their customers."

That picture is still on my shelf, and visitors often ask about it.

If you're at a trade show, you can create your own event within the event. Take your booth and make an event out of it. Invite people to come and get their picture taken with the CEO or with some celebrity. (You'd be surprised how inexpensive some well-known celebs are for such events!) Send your visitors home with the picture as a souvenir. One of the things I've learned is people *love* having their picture taken with somebody else. Even today, with our digital phones, people still love to have pictures on their wall or on their shelves.

I learned this the hard way. Many years ago, my last real job was working for a Japanese company, long before digital arrived. My boss and I traveled around the world, visiting our distributors and agents. He kept having me take his picture with them, wherever we went. I thought it was stupid. When we got back, he had them developed and framed, and he sent them out to everybody. The next time I went on the road and visited these people on my own, *almost all of them* had that picture on their wall or on a shelf somewhere. Boy, was I way off!

Even in the digital present, when I go to people's offices, there are always pictures. Most of the time they're of their families, but not always. I'll see photos that show them with someone else at an event, and inevitably I ask, "Hey, who's that?" And the answer is something like, "Oh, that's Steve! He supplies me with . . ." and that starts a referral conversation for you.

Charity events are great ways to do well while doing good. I have a very good friend, Jeff, who is a property developer. Jeff is active with several local charities, but he's especially involved with the Big Brothers/Big Sisters organization. He's on the board of directors, and he's the primary sponsor of the organization's golf tournament every year. Now, he is absolutely 100 percent genuine in his support of the cause. But he's not stupid. He's also a businessman, and so he recognizes that at these events, not only will he be introduced by the head of the charity to other people at the event but also, when the time comes for the speeches thanking the big donors, his name will be called out to much applause.

You can take advantage of these kinds of face-to-face events in many different ways to create direct or indirect referrals, as long as you're Uncopyable. There can only be one title sponsor of the Big Brothers/Big Sisters golf tournament, and my friend Jeff is that guy.

If I've got a photo op in my booth, and someone else tries to do the same thing, they're copying me and everyone's going to know it.

4. Throw Out Your Boring Business Card and Get an Uncopyable One.

When I speak to business people about being Uncopyable and explain to them the objective is to separate themselves from their competition, almost everybody will tell me, "Well, we *are* different from the competition." I'll say, "Really? You're different? Show me your business card."

They take out their card, and 99 percent of the time, it looks exactly like everybody else's business card.

Can I let you in on a secret? My friend, your card is your *number-one* personal-marketing tool, the one physical thing you are going to hand out to all prospects. Other than your being face-to-face with them, this card represents you more often than anything else. And if you say you're different but you hand out a business card that looks the same as everybody else's, you have automatically negated what you're saying. You have to walk the talk.

For example, on the back of my business card, a couple of gender-neutral cartoon characters are pictured. One is saying, "Are you mentally undressing me?" The other replies, "No, I'm mentally marketing myself." On the flip side, the card reads, "Steve Miller. Kelly's Dad, Marketing Gunslinger." It's completely Uncopyable, unique to me, and people notice. When I go to a convention where I've previously spoken, somebody will inevitably come up to me with someone else in tow and say, "This is the guy whose business card I showed you."

When this happens, I always hand out a couple of extra cards and say, "Glad you like 'em. Here you go. Show them to your friends." I'm not explicitly asking them for referrals. I'm giving them something that's fun and worth sharing. They'll share my card because it's out of the ordinary—and Uncopyable.

5. Write a Book.

Besides my business card, the single best example of a great referral tool I can give is a book I've written myself. A book builds credibility, authority, and confidence. It carries an invisible power!

You're reading my book right now. I promise you my sincere objective is to provide you with a new perspective on marketing, as well as a set of tools you can use to separate your company from the competition.

And I'm in business, just like you. So when you have a marketing/branding issue, or need a speaker for your next event, I hope this book stimulates you to think of me!

A book is an amazing marketing tool. It's also an amazing referral-marketing tool. When my first book came out twenty-seven years ago, I didn't just give autographed copies of my book to my clients. If you were a client of mine, I'd give you *three* autographed copies. The first one was inscribed personally for you, and the other two were simply signed. I would say, "Here are two extra signed copies, my gift to you. If you meet somebody or you're talking to somebody whom you think this book would help, please give a copy as your gift." Of course, my way-cool business card was inside each book.

Does this work? Brilliantly. If you've got someone in your office who is saying, "Man, I really wish I could come up with some kind of system that helps me to separate myself from the competition," you're going to say, "You know what? I've got this guy I work with, Steve Miller. He has this great system we've been using, and he wrote this terrific book about it. In fact, you know what? I've got an extra copy. Let me give it to you."

That's an endorsed referral. *And it's painless.* I'm not even in the room.

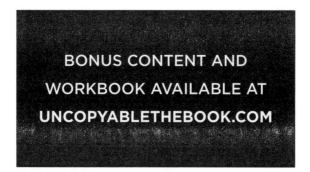

CHAPTER EIGHT

The Rules

Before I get into this chapter, I want to stress something important. I'm not one of those consultants or speakers who says, "My way is the only way to do this."

My philosophy is there are many roads to the top of the mountain. What I've shared with you is the road that's worked for me and my clients. I think it will work for you.

That said, I am going to share with you seven rules I believe are critical to a quest to be Uncopyable. These seven rules establish an Uncopyable positioning and an Uncopyable Attachment to people. You need to track and follow these rules as closely as possible. In fact, I'd go so far as to say some of these rules are absolute and immutable and not even up for discussion. A couple of the rules are a bit more flexible, but if you truly want to create Uncopyable Attachment, then the more closely you follow these tenets, the better. Remember being Uncopyable is about breaking the mold, not just retrofitting it or painting it a different color.

1. Look At What Everybody Else Is Doing, and Don't Do It.

Sit down right now with a piece of paper and a pencil. Draw a line down the middle. On the left side, write down all the reasons why you think people should do business with you. On the right side, write down all the reasons your competitors would say people should do business with *them*.

Okay, now go back and read them all. If you've written the same thing on both sides, at any point, cross those reasons off.

Now, look for things on your side that are *not* on your competitors' side. Those are the areas you're going to focus on because *they're unique to you.*

The worst thing you can do is follow the follower all the time. Yeah, there are certain things you have to do to maintain a level of competitiveness with them, but you're better off if you zig when they zag. If someone says green is the hot new color, so everything needs to be green, your instinct has to tell you to flip and say that everything's going to be orange—because you are not going to do what *they* do.

2. There Will Always Be a Next Step.

This goes back into chapter two's Marketing Diamond, but this rule means that whatever you are doing has to be designed so as to proactively encourage your marketplace to go to the next step.

When you think about your brand—the experience, the tools, or Stealing Genius—you are not using those things to build awareness, because you cannot cash a check on awareness.

It's sort of like the physician's rule that prescription before diagnosis is malpractice. Awareness without persuasion is also malpractice. The idea of persuasion is to recognize that whatever you're doing, there's a next step in the process you want to have happen.

That's why there's always a persuasion component. I call this *next-step marketing*. Let me share a couple of examples of what I mean by next-step marketing:

- Let's say your company will be exhibiting at the industry's big trade show in a couple of months. You know a smart thing to do is create a preshow communication campaign to promote your exhibit. So what is the *next* step here? It's not to promote how great your products and company are; it's to get people to *stop* in your booth. Nothing happens until a qualified moose stops.

- Another example is direct mail. If you send a mailing out to a large group of prospects, what's the *next* step? It's to get them to *open* the mailing. If they don't open the mailing, they'll never see the sales message inside.

Always look ahead to what that next step is and think of how can you use your tools to move people to that next step.

3. It's Much Better to Be a Big Fish in a Small-but-Rich Pond Than It Is to Be a Small Fish in a Big Pond.

Clearly, this is not rocket science, but the idea is if you can be Uncopyable in a small-but-rich pond, it's much easier for you to protect that territory. And it's much easier to get your customers or prospects into your club. If you've got a few thousand potential customers, it's far less challenging to separate yourself from the competition than to try to compete with companies in a marketplace that has millions of prospects. That's why I always encourage my clients to be big fish.

4. This Is Not "Set It and Forget It."

By that I mean that, literally, *on a daily basis,* you have to be looking for fresh new ways to communicate how you are Uncopyable. You're looking for an innovative approach to providing anchors and triggers to people, every single day.

Nothing stays fresh and surprising indefinitely, no matter how groundbreaking it was at its inception. People and companies forget that at their peril. Take a typical company website: a company might invest a ton of money in building and developing its website, and then it's done for five years. Sure, it all looks innovative and cool when it's first created, but after a couple of years, it's gone stale.

The same rule applies in the Uncopyable world. What is Uncopyable today is not going to be Uncopyable in two or three years, so you have to always be looking to push the envelope. *Nothing,* no matter how up-to-the-minute or brilliant it is, is going to stay Uncopyable forever.

5. You Are Not a Business Doing Business with Businesses. You Are Always a Human Doing Business with Humans.

Although most of my clients are in the B2B world, I find even in the B2C world, businesses still tend to think of themselves as businesses. But your consumers, or whoever your buyers are, don't think of themselves as a business. They think of themselves as human beings, and so must you.

Even if you're, technically, a business doing business with businesses, you're still dealing with human beings. People go to movies, have kids and grandkids, drive cars, and go to church. They're people, just like anybody else. So you're always humans doing business with humans, and you always need to be thinking about your business that way and speaking to your customers and prospects that way.

In the B2C world, you wouldn't think, for example, *Oh, I'm Coca-Cola communicating with Steve.* You can't do that. Even if you're employed by Coca-Cola, you still have to think like a human who is communicating with humans.

6. Look to Be Controversial.

This is something that scares people, but it's absolutely critical that you're willing to risk skating on the edge here. Why? Because if you're not a little bit controversial, if you're not pushing the envelope on some level, then you're almost certainly too easy to copy.

Being Uncopyable means—*should* mean—you are not for everybody. Being a little bit controversial thins the herd. People who are not like you, people who don't think like you, are probably people you don't want to do business with anyway.

People don't talk about ordinary experiences. You never hear people tell stories about how their expectations were met, right? You only hear about their experiences when they've sucked,

BEING UNCOPYABLE MEANS—*SHOULD* MEAN—YOU ARE NOT FOR EVERYBODY.

or when they're amazing. That's where the idea of being controversial comes in because people talk about it—and it makes it easier for them to remember you.

Remember the groundbreaking Calvin Klein jeans ad of 1980, featuring a very young Brooke Shields cooing, "Nothing comes between me and my Calvins"? If you're old enough, I'm guessing you do. Clearly, these were not your grandma's jeans, but your grandma wasn't the audience they were selling to. The ads shocked a lot of people and generated controversy and conversations. But the audience they wanted to sell to loved them, and Calvin Klein sold a *lot* of jeans. That was a fearless and brilliant use of creating controversy to set their brand apart, and it was truly Uncopyable.

And I don't think I have to convince you Donald Trump ran a very controversial campaign for president!

7. Remember What You're Really Selling Is Attachment and the Experience People Have with You.

The product you deliver is merely the souvenir, the tangible piece they can show to say, "This is what I paid to have delivered." But, in reality, what they're paying for is the value of their connection with your company, which is much, much higher than a mere product's.

———

Every moving part—from Uncopyable branding to creating Uncopyable experiences to Stealing Genius to creating rock stars—works in concert. Every piece of the puzzle connects to the next.

This business of making yourself Uncopyable is kind of like a magic trick. I never get tired of performing it for my clients because their response is a lot like seeing me pull a rabbit out of my hat; it's full of wide eyes, "oohs," and "aaahs." And that's great fun, but my real mission is to show them and you how the trick is done so they and you can do it too.

BONUS CONTENT AND
WORKBOOK AVAILABLE AT
UNCOPYABLETHEBOOK.COM

In the beginning of this book, I stated the obvious: *Because competition is fierce, you must be Unocpyable.*

You *must* separate yourself from the competition not just by being better but also by being *different.* Better is important, but it is almost always copyable—more sooner than later. Different can be Uncopyable, and it can be defensible.

Although this book has been primarily aimed at small businesses, the concept of achieving Uncopyable Superiority is applicable to all organizations.

For example, when is a university not a university?

Have you ever heard of the Disneyland of Universities? That title was bestowed upon High Point University by the British newspaper, the *Daily Mail.*[15]

High Point University (HPU) is located in High Point, North Carolina. Established as a liberal arts school in 1924, HPU has forty-eight undergraduate majors, fifty-one undergraduate minors, and thirteen graduate-degree majors.

"America's Best Colleges" 2017 edition, published in the *U.S. News & World Report*, ranks HPU number one among all regional

---

15   Sara Malm, "Is this the best university you've never heard of? The $700 million Disney-style campus complete with an ice cream truck, a movie theatre… and Skee ball!" *Daily Mail,* January 10, 2014, http://www.dailymail.co.uk/news/article-2537212/Is-best-university-youve-never-heard-The-700-million-Disney-style-campus-complete-ice-cream-truck-movie-theatre-Skee-ball.html#ixzz4QMt47Hb1.

colleges in the South (the fifth consecutive year at number one) and number one for the most innovative regional college in the South (the second consecutive year at number one).

In 2005, Dr. Nido Qubein was named as the new president of High Point University. I'm happy and proud to say Nido is a friend of mine. We first met in 1986 through the National Speakers Association.

Nido is a successful businessman, speaker, and author. He is not a college administrator.

Shortly after Nido took the reins at HPU, I took my "club" for a visit. The campus and enrollment was small, but Nido had big plans. He shared with us a vision for enormous change and advancement for HPU, not only making it a world-class educational facility but enhancing the overall student experience and preparation for lifetime success, as well.

Since 2005, HPU's extraordinary transformation is almost hard to fathom:

- an increase from 1,450 to 4,500 students

- an increase in the number of faculty from 108 to 300

- the addition of 90 new and acquired buildings on campus

- a total investment of over *one billion dollars*[16]

When my club returned in 2014 for an update visit, we were stunned by what we saw. The beautiful campus had obviously expanded tremendously, including perks and benefits like a free first-run movie theater, a free ice-cream truck, and dorms with plasma-screen TVs, outdoor hot tubs, and concierges. But it was the student "learning experience" we were most impressed with. Let me share just a couple of examples.

---

16   "Office of the President," High Point University, http://www.highpoint.edu/president/.

Incoming freshmen are required to attend a course titled "The President's Seminar on Life Skills." Presented by Nido, he covers essential skills needed after college that are rarely covered by traditional higher institutions, such as how to gain positive self-esteem, the art and science of goal setting, the basics of time management, the importance of fiscal literacy, and how to make persuasive presentations.

Each of the school buildings has a "presentation" room designed to stage an experience much like you would have in the real business world. When students are assigned a presentation, the class moves to one of those rooms. The Plato S. Wilson School of Commerce includes a full-size replica of a financial trading floor.

1924 Prime is a first-class steakhouse on campus, much like a Morton's or Ruth's Chris. Students are allowed to eat there once a week as part of their paid student-meal program. But it's not just a top-drawer meal. 1924 Prime is also a learning laboratory. First, there's a dress code. For gentlemen, a collared shirt, dress slacks or khakis, and dress shoes or loafers are required. For ladies, a dress, skirt, or dress pants are required. Jeans, flip-flops, and tennis shoes are prohibited for both. During meals, students are exposed to proper social and dining etiquette. There is also a Cuisine & Culture Series, exposing students to distinct international and regional cuisines and culture from the different locations.

Through Nido's leadership, High Point University has clearly built its own box, embracing many of the Uncopyable strategies I've outlined:

- a strong branding proposition

- triggers and anchors

- shock-and-awe gifts (I've personally received several after participating in on-campus programs with Nido.)

- creating a club students want to be a part of (I want to go back to school there!)

- creating an amazing and Uncopyable student experience

When is a trade show not a trade show? When it's the International Manufacturing Technology Show (IMTS).

Do most trade shows you attend look exactly alike? Big banners welcoming you to the National Widget Expo, same old, same old registration areas, cavernous halls filled with row upon row of exhibitors shouting for you to buy their products?

Not IMTS.

Owned and produced by the Association for Manufacturing Technology, IMTS is held every two years at the vast McCormick Place convention center in Chicago, Illinois. One of the largest events in the world, the 2016 IMTS had 115,612 total attendees, 1.37 million net square feet of exhibit space, and 2,407 exhibiting companies.

What makes IMTS Uncopyable is its unmatched commitment to both attendees and exhibitors.

Instead of just a giant banner to welcome attendees, they have a custom hot-air balloon floating in front of the main entrance to McCormick Place. When people see the balloon, they know they're at IMTS.

Outside the exhibit floors, IMTS features highly interesting and engaging displays sharing the past, the present, and the future of manufacturing technology. Before 3-D printing ("additive manufacturing" as it's known in the industry) became a buzzword for all of us, IMTS's Emerging Technology Center printed the world's first working *car*, dubbed the Strati. On day one, all that existed were four tires and an electric engine. A giant Cincinnati Incorporated machine worked twenty-four hours a day for the six days of the show, creating an ongoing *wow* for all attendees. On day six, the Strati drove off the show floor and took a lap around McCormick Place.

At other locations in the convention center, IMTS has featured a full-scale replica of the Wright Brothers airplane, an Airbus H130 seven-person helicopter, a full fuselage of the Boeing 787, and a Lockheed Martin F-35 Lightning II Joint Strike Fighter aircraft.

IMTS embraces the *create rock stars* philosophy by featuring industry stakeholders in their communications and promotions. These rock stars are interviewed and featured prominently on graphics throughout the event.

IMTS has its own TV channel running online throughout the year, but even bigger; they have a full-size studio onsite during the event.

Exhibiting at trade shows is a very different type of go-to market tool. While providing face-to-face contact, they are expensive and, quite frankly, time consuming for corporations looking for new business. Since 1984, IMTS has committed itself to help exhibitors maximize their investment by providing extensive education utilizing the best resources in the world. Six months before every event, IMTS puts on a free two-day workshop for exhibitors covering all aspects of marketing and operations.

In addition, IMTS provides monthly educational webinars and podcasts for both exhibitors and professional attendees with topics covering marketing, branding, business growth, industry outlook, and trends.

So what's my point here? Harley-Davidson is just a motorcycle. Space Mountain is just a roller coaster. Incisive Computing is just a software company. High Point University is just a college. And IMTS is just a trade show.

In their essence, each one of these examples is a highly common product or service. Each of their respective markets is overflowing with competition. But each one of these has embraced the concept of looking for strategies and tactics that not only clearly *separate* them from the competition but also create *attachment* with targeted stakeholders.

They have built their own boxes. They are *Uncopyable*.

You should notice, though, every one of my examples in this book uses different parts of the Uncopyable strategies and tools I've shared. You don't have to use them all. In fact, for most of my corporate clients, I recommend using only a handful. Look through these ideas and select one or two that resonate for you.

I'll leave you with one of my all time favorite quotes from Frank Perdue of Perdue Farms:

> *If you can differentiate a dead chicken,*
> *you can differentiate anything.*

Now, go be Uncopyable.

ABOUT THE AUTHOR

Meetings & Conventions magazine calls Steve Miller the "Idea Man" for his nontraditional approach to marketing and branding.

Steve calls himself *Kelly's Dad*. That's who he *is*. His business title is *Marketing Gunslinger*. He helps businesses grow by achieving what he calls "*Uncopyable Superiority.*"

Steve is an author, a professional speaker, and a business advisor known for his edgy, no-spin-zone perspective. He's the son of the coinventor of the 8-track; he played on the PGA Tour, worked in the copper mines of Arizona, and even worked in Hollywood (all of which means he's basically unemployable).

Since founding The Adventure LLC in 1984, Steve's consulting clients have ranged from solo entrepreneurs to Fortune 100 megacorporations, including Proctor & Gamble (advising on the Swiffer WetJet product launch), Boeing Commercial Airplane (the 777 launch), Nordstrom, Starbucks, Caterpillar, Philips Electronics, Coca-Cola, and Halliburton, to name a few. He has also consulted for most of North America's largest exhibitions, including CONEXPO-CON/AGG, the International Manufacturing Technology Show, the International Home & Housewares Show, the Work Truck Show, AAPEX, and the Sweets & Snacks Expo.

Steve has presented over *1,500 speeches and workshops* around the world for corporations and trade associations in *126 different industries*, including the prestigious main TED Conference.

Besides his seven books, Steve has written for and been featured in over 250 publications, including *Fast Company, Business Week, Fortune, the Wall Street Journal, the Washington Post, Success, Association Management,* and *Highlights for Children.* (Okay, he made that last one up.)

To learn how your organization can become Uncopyable or to have Steve speak at your next meeting or event, contact:

The Adventure LLC

T: 253-874-9665

TheAdventure.com